From **Onboarding** to **Everboarding**

Redefining Employee Development

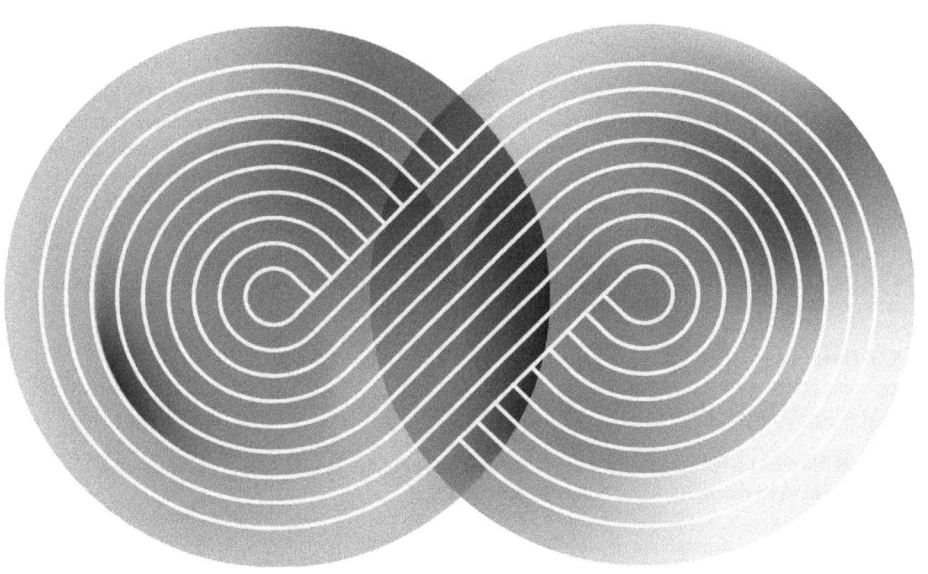

Amber Watts

PRESS
Alexandria, VA

© 2025 ASTD DBA the Association for Talent Development (ATD)
All rights reserved.

28 27 26 25   1 2 3 4 5

No part of this publication may be reproduced, distributed, or transmitted in any form or by any means, including photocopying, recording, information storage and retrieval systems, or other electronic or mechanical methods, without the prior written permission of the publisher, except in the case of brief quotations embodied in critical reviews and certain other noncommercial uses permitted by copyright law. For permission requests, please go to copyright.com, or contact Copyright Clearance Center (CCC), 222 Rosewood Drive, Danvers, MA 01923 (telephone: 978.750.8400; fax: 978.646.8600).

ATD Press is an internationally renowned source of insightful and practical information on talent development, training, and professional development.

ATD Press
1640 King Street
Alexandria, VA 22314 USA

Ordering information: Books published by ATD Press can be purchased by visiting ATD's website at td.org/books or by calling 800.628.2783 or 703.683.8100.

Library of Congress Control Number: 2025934708

ISBN-10: 1-96023-128-6
ISBN-13: 978-1-960231-28-4
e-ISBN: 978-1-96023-129-1

ATD Press Editorial Staff
Director: Sarah Halgas
Manager: Melissa Jones
Content Manager: Mallory Flynn
Developmental Editor: Jack Harlow
Production Editor: Katy Wiley Stewts
Text Designer: Shirley E.M. Raybuck
Cover Designer: Rose Richey

More Praise for *From Onboarding to Everboarding*

"This book is a must-read for leaders who want to create a culture of continuous growth and development. It provides a strategic, scalable approach to keeping employees engaged beyond their first few weeks—exactly what modern organizations need." —**Ryan Austin,** Founder and CEO, Cognota

"Amber Watts brilliantly highlights the importance of continuous learning and reinforcement in today's fast-changing world. This book shows how everboarding is not only the future of onboarding, but also the key to thriving in dynamic workplaces. It's not a question of if you will embrace everboarding, but when." —**Melanie Fellay,** Co-Founder and CEO, Spekit

"I've seen firsthand how effective onboarding can shorten new-hire ramp times and improve production. I've also seen how engaging managers and fostering employees to own their development can create a cadence of continuous improvement that lifts performance across a sales force. In her book, Amber tackles all angles with proven, effective advice that every sales leader and enablement professional should adopt. Buy it, read it, apply it." —**Mike Kunkle,** Vice President, Sales Effectiveness Services, SPARXiQ; Author, *The Building Blocks of Sales Enablement*

"Forget onboarding that stops at week 2—this book delivers a masterclass in making employee development a lifelong VIP experience. With a smart blend of strategy, psychology, and just the right dose of 'Why didn't we always do it this way?' everboarding transforms talent development from a checkbox into a culture. A must-read for anyone serious about retention, growth, and finally getting employee engagement right." —**Cara North,** Vice President, HR Product Management, JP Morgan Chase

"*From Onboarding to Everboarding* flips the script on how we bring people into the fold—it's not about endless training; it's about nurturing confident, capable team members who grow and contribute well beyond day one. With wit, wisdom, and plenty of real talk, this book is a must for leaders ready to evolve their approach." —**Kassy LaBorie,** Keynote Speaker and Author of *Interact and Engage! 75+ Activities for Virtual Training, Meetings, and Webinars*

"Brimming with smart, timely strategies, this book ensures employees get the development they need—right when they need it. Everboarding is your answer to talent development's ever-evolving needs to support our ever-growing organizations in an ever-changing world. This isn't just about 24/7 access to learning—it's a transformative, ongoing approach that equips every employee to meet your organization's ever-shifting demands." —**Elaine Biech,** ISA Thought Leader; Author, *The Art and Science of Training*

Contents

Introduction v

Chapter 1. Everboarding as a Must-Have Strategy 1

Part 1. Training-Led Onboarding
Chapter 2. Establishing Support Systems 21
Chapter 3. Making Onboarding Personal 35
Chapter 4. Tapping Mentors as Your Partners in Onboarding 45
Chapter 5. Celebrating Milestones Over Graduations 53

Part 2. Manager-Led Development
Chapter 6. Securing Manager Involvement 69
Chapter 7. Preparing Your Managers 83
Chapter 8. Evaluating New-Hire Success 89
Chapter 9. Equipping Managers for Ongoing Support 107

Part 3. Employee-Led Refinement
Chapter 10. Creating an Environment for Self-Led Learning 119
Chapter 11. Recognizing Continuous Growth 127
Chapter 12. Bringing in Current Employees 135

Conclusion. The Everboarding Difference 145

Appendix. Case Studies
Heritage Communities 150
Data Axle 154
Nokia 159

References 163

Index 165

About the Author 171

About ATD 173

Introduction

Back in 2016, I was working for a large healthcare staffing company that had a reputation for an outstanding onboarding program. My team had won a BEST Award from ATD, been recognized as one of *Training* magazine's Top 125 winners (now Apex Awards), and granted a Best Places to Work Sustained Excellence Award. We were confident that our workplace learning efforts were perpetually great.

Our onboarding program was a well-oiled machine, and senior executives not only sponsored it, they also actively participated. We were intentional about assessing new hires' progress, gathering their individual feedback, and coaching them one on one, each week for 13 weeks. Once a new hire successfully completed their formal training, they received college credit with a local university. Our industry-recognized onboarding program helped us secure top talent. Looking back, I believe that what ultimately made the onboarding program so successful was the alignment we had with our people managers and the carefully selected mentors. Everyone was drinking the onboarding Kool-Aid, including myself.

Then, a new team formed within the company. They needed training content for current and future employees, so I began to closely partner with them. All their current employees had previously benefited from our successful onboarding program. One had even been a Rising Star recipient—an award given to the top-performing new hire. But, as the months passed by, I grew concerned about their team's knowledge of relevant, up-to-date strategies and industry changes. Specifically, employees seemed to have taken two steps backward in their performance between months four and 12. When I initially brought this concern up, I was told that "it's typical for employees here and they'll turn it around." Well, the next logical question I asked myself was, "If that's typical, why aren't we solving for it?" It became glaringly obvious to me that their professional development ended the day an employee graduated from onboarding. It's best described as booting them off the metaphorical cliff without a parachute and their manager waiting for them at the bottom. I knew there had to be a better way.

From that experience, my first attempt at everboarding was born—I used to label it "postgrad training" and "monthly refreshers." Identifying topics and skills for these new ideas was not easy because my organization wasn't actively capturing that data. I had to go directly to the source: the people. Over the course of several months, I interviewed branch managers, team leaders, regional managers, employees between four and 12 months of tenure, and the L&D team. My goal was to get a very granular understanding of gaps in workflows and skills learned in onboarding. Patterns emerged and I was able to identify what dropped off at each month of tenure. From there, I put together a training schedule for months four through 12 to try to combat the forgetting curve. I created monthly refreshers to alleviate resistance toward adopting new business processes and technology. The first monthly refresher was also the first time my team used virtual training technology to reach employees at all locations.

Leadership had been extremely supportive of the onboarding program, which led me to assume they would be supportive of these two initiatives. While the monthly refreshers were well supported and well attended, postgrad training received resistance. Leaders didn't want to allow their employees to head back to the training room once a month for more development until they reached one year of employment. In their minds, the employees were on the typical trajectory, and I had not yet convinced them that there could be a better way. It took time to gain alignment and a path forward that better prepared the newest employees, but once we did, we saw a ripple effect. The employees participating in postgrad training were elevating the employees in our onboarding program and also teaching their tenured teammates new, improved ways to do things.

The virtual refreshers were going so well that we shifted the postgrad training to virtual—and that one change put many managers' minds at ease. No longer was I requiring their employees to travel to other locations, reducing the time away from their desk. Looking back, I think the shift from opposition to acceptance can be attributed to manager inclusion. We had never formally trained employees past onboarding, and the trust to do so was not yet established. Luckily, a manager shared this with me and I was able to adjust my approach and give them a louder voice in their respective market.

My time in that role allowed me to test these ideas out and bring the concept of everboarding to future workplaces. The industries and products changed, but the need to remove onboarding's exit day remains everywhere I have led learning. Year after year, I have evolved everboarding into a holistic talent strategy by removing outdated practices such as new-hire graduations. That strategy is now fully baked and ready to be shared in a way that you can actually reheat and serve to your own team and organization.

What Is Everboarding?

In many ways, I was advocating for everboarding even before I realized I was doing it. And now, I've become a full-blown advocate of this approach to employee development. I have led workplace learning at an HR software company, a data and marketing company, and a global hospitality software company. I've also worked as a consultant, but bringing the everboarding approach hasn't been easy and it's often required level setting with organizational leaders and managers about what it is and isn't. For example, when I was working for a global hospitality software company, the chief revenue officer (CRO) warned me: "Amber, this is something my prior Fortune 500 company wasn't even doing. I'd love to support this, but do we really have the resources to do it?" I'll never forget that. But, we didn't need the technology, people power, or budget that those companies have to be successful, and it took me one conversation (and a lot of preparation ahead of time) to help them see that.

The dominant challenge I faced was that very few companies have an established onboarding program, let alone something resembling an everboarding strategy. As a consultant for Spekit, I spoke with learning leaders at companies of all sizes and in various industries. I learned only one of them had a continuous learning strategy in place, but even their onboarding program was brief and impersonal. Despite these differences, they all had one thing in common: Every learning leader saw the value in elevating their managers' people development skills and wanted to take the steps to implement an everboarding strategy.

When I advocate for everboarding, however, I often hear some common objections and misconceptions:

- It's the flavor of the month.
- It's more training and we don't have that kind of time or budget to support it.
- It's just extending our onboarding program, and new hires need to be ramped up by week two so we can start our next class.
- It's more content and we don't have time for that because we just lost half our team due to layoffs.
- We don't have time, we don't have time, we don't have time.

Before I offer my explanation of everboarding, think about your perception of it. Is it a talent program within your workplace? Would you consider it a new training methodology? Or do you think it's like riding an impossibly long skateboard? Just picture it: If you start your journey now and all goes well, you might make it to the end before skinny jeans make their next comeback. In all seriousness, it's none of those (although the last one is the most plausible).

Often, these misconceptions occur because we're thinking of everboarding as something that it's not. The word *everboarding* itself is autological; it combines the words onboarding and evergreen—meaning, learning has no end. At its core, *everboarding* is a strategy that supports all your talent management programs from acquisition to succession planning. Unfortunately, I continue to see it being marketed as a continuation of onboarding, and if that's the approach you choose to believe and take, it will not transform your organization.

I've discovered through my networking, speaking, and consulting experiences that most organizations spend around two weeks onboarding employees and offer little support thereafter. You might be thinking that it depends on the role. And, you're right; onboarding timelines are role dependent, but everboarding removes that dependency. When employees are given an abrupt end to training and left to go it alone, they will consume misinformation and develop poor habits, or worse they will fail. The model in Figure I-1 compares traditional onboarding to everboarding. Use it to envision how everboarding supports your employees on their entire journey from becoming top performers, moving into new roles, preparing for promotions, overcoming performance gaps, and eventually offboarding.

Figure I-1.
Comparison of Traditional Onboarding and Everboarding Approaches

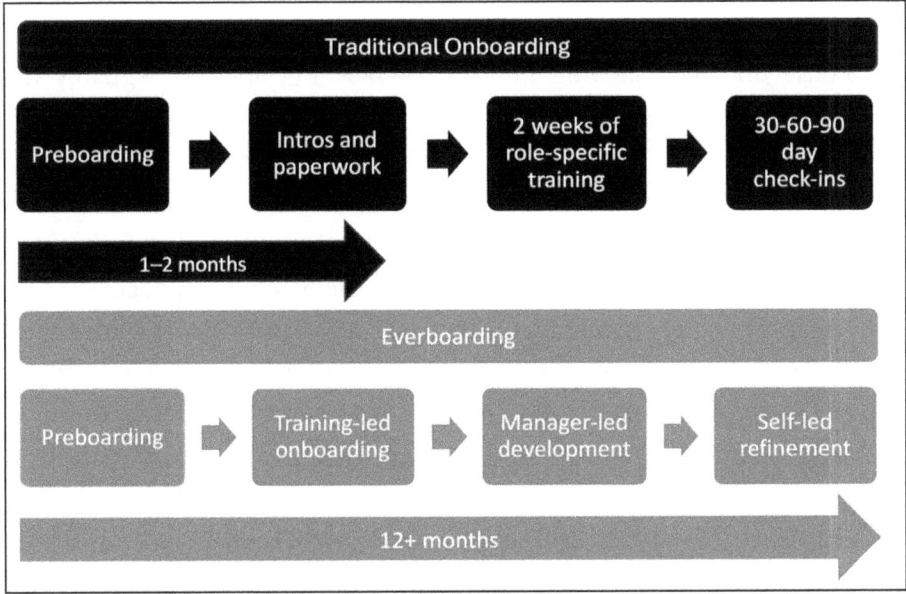

In this book, you'll learn that onboarding is only the first phase—the launch phase—in a three-phase everboarding strategy. You'll learn how keeping new hires in training is not the answer. Creating more content for them to consume and providing accompanying formal assessments to pass will cause resistance among employees. In my experience, everboarding works best if we treat it like a strategy or a science. Only then will it be scalable, measurable, and sustainable.

This book offers a deep dive into the three-phase everboarding strategy that you can incorporate into any organization of any size and industry, with quick actions to start implementing it. Whether you have robust learning programs in place or are just beginning to formalize learning in your workplace, this strategy is flexible to fit your team and your unique needs. To demonstrate that, I'll share three case studies from companies that have adopted this approach to employee development.

Have you heard the overused phrase, "It's a marathon, not a sprint"? Well, everboarding is neither—it's more like a relay. Each talent management function carries the baton and onboarding is your first runner. Whether a team or an individual owns these functions, sometimes in silos, they all receive support from this new strategy.

Phase one—the starting line—is onboarding, and it's arguably the most important phase of everboarding. It sets the tone for what learning in your workplace feels like! We will discuss the importance of creating a charter and how it will set you up for everboarding success. Expect to learn new best practices, ways to assess onboarding effectiveness, who the key players are, and how to seamlessly pass the baton to managers.

Phase two—the middle leg—involves diving into the role managers play in employees' development and how the talent development team can prepare them to run with the baton. A manager's ability to coach and develop their employees will make or break your everboarding strategy. Without proper training and resources to support them, managers can't support their employees. Expect to learn why managers are truly the cornerstone of employee success and your most valuable ally in all things learning and performance. Whether you're reviewing assessments, coaching models, or toolkits, you'll want a highlighter handy for the chapters in this phase.

Phase three—the final leg—is the refinement phase of your everboarding strategy. It will help you ensure consistency across your organization, as well as inspire and influence a culture of self-led learning. The world is evolving and your reinforcement efforts must be along for the ride. This part is full of tips on how to continuously support employees in a hybrid environment and how to bring current employees into the fold. (I promise to provide better folding directions than an episode of *Schitt's Creek*: "Just . . . fold them in.")

The Benefits of Everboarding

According to ATD's 2023 research report *Building a Strong Organizational Culture*, training and facilitation efforts (83 percent) and onboarding programs (70 percent) had the most positive impact on organizational culture. Onboarding is the time to introduce new hires to your company's values and culture, and failure to convey these elements leads to misalignment and lack of engagement in continuous learning. If you are reading this book, you likely know how a lack of training and onboarding can negatively influence your organization's culture. You care deeply about employee development past onboarding and are wondering how an everboarding strategy can integrate with your current talent management efforts.

An everboarding strategy has several benefits compared with an onboarding-only approach to employee development or with a disjointed onboarding and occasional training experience:

1. **Engagement.** You'll see an increase in employees' engagement with their work, their team, and the organization when they feel confident and supported with the right tools and resources throughout their entire employee life cycle.
2. **Acquisition.** Help your recruiting team land top talent with a message to candidates that says, "We care about your success here and we will invest in it beyond orientation."
3. **Succession planning.** A safe environment for ongoing development supports a strong internal bench to face the growing skills gaps in your organization.
4. **Performance support.** You can now help employees achieve mastery because onboarding alone can't.

Everboarding is gaining momentum and it's no surprise why. The way we've always done things is no longer working, especially in a world with virtual and hybrid workplaces. Additionally, we've witnessed the Great

Resignation, quiet quitting, and quiet hiring, and we're left to navigate the mess they've left in our workplaces. The demand for a new way, like everboarding, is flooding our newsfeeds and inboxes with numerous thought leadership articles, sponsored webinars, and learning technology companies rebranding their go-to-market messaging. Yet, I bet you still don't have a robust plan for how to make this change. This book couldn't be more timely. I will debunk the myths and misconceptions around everboarding and give you a path to application.

The more L&D professionals I've shared the concepts in this book with, the more confident I am in the impact it will have on the workplace. Recently, I presented a one-hour virtual program about implementing an everboarding strategy to a local ATD chapter. A concept like this takes time to gain buy-in and shift the mindset across the organization, but a week later, I received an email from a participant stating that they were making progress! Not only were they tossing out the two-day orientation they currently offered to anyone who wasn't sales, they added a new role to their team because their senior leader could see the value in ongoing development. With the addition of this new role (an employee development specialist), they will be able to devote time to developing employees outside sales for the first time. This person, in partnership with the curator on their team, will support a powerful ongoing development experience.

Do You Want to Redefine Employee Development?

If you believe that onboarding in your workplace needs to be revolutionized, this book is for you. You are the voice, the pioneer who can influence your team and your organization to embrace this strategy as a new, better path forward. Imagine a workplace where employees are constantly improving their skills and embracing new challenges with confidence. You can create that reality, but not without allies.

According to research conducted by Gallup (n.d.), only 29 percent of employees say they feel fully prepared and supported to excel in their role after their onboarding experience. Two-thirds of employees are left with doubt and uncertainty. They're wondering if they will succeed or receive any support they might need. If you want to have stellar employees, they need to have stellar development.

I can't accompany you to your strategy meetings and get your team on board with everboarding, but I can provide what you need to build your business case. With this book as your talent strategy GPS, you can create the people-centric approach that our industry is evolving toward.

"Courage is the root of change—and change is what we're chemically designed to do." —Bonnie Garmus, *Lessons in Chemistry* (2022)

Are you ready to inspire self-led, continuous learning in your workplace? Tie your laces and grab your baton. Your everboarding journey has just begun. *starting pistol shoots off*

CHAPTER 1
Everboarding as a Must-Have Strategy

Everboarding Myth #1
Everboarding is a continuation of onboarding.

Learning at work is a fundamental need that all employees must receive support with. Building a culture of learning requires psychological safety and the ability to fail without consequence. Having one indicates that your team is full of curiosity. However, learning is not an indicator of success, and simply having a culture of learning is not the end result of an everboarding strategy, as it is often presumed to be.

Rather, everboarding creates a culture of growth. When you integrate your learning initiatives with your other talent management initiatives, such as performance management, you foster a culture of growth in which success is measured by progress and improvement, not just a willingness to learn.

Getting Involved

As the world rapidly changes, talent development must keep up with the demand within our business, and the only way you can be aware of each team's unique needs is to be closely involved. Be a partner and an ally to guide the leaders of your organization. You don't need to have all the answers to their challenges, but you can partner to help them uncover those answers.

Everboarding is not a formal learning program. It is an effort to continue the conversations, the collaboration happening on and off teams, the allyship with frontline managers, and a support system for your senior leaders to see their change initiatives followed through. Don't simply rely on your training intake process—be proactive and suggest training or other development solutions where you see gaps!

There are many ways in which your team can make itself an available partner in new initiatives. Here are some I've seen work well:

1. **Offer to be a part of a technology evaluation.** Someone on your team is considered an expert in a current solution and knows the user experience well because of the feedback they get during training. They can help stakeholders compare options.

2. **If your talent acquisition team is revamping the hiring experience, offer to be a part of it.** Someone on your team can share what a new hire can expect in the first 30 days on the job, which is a common question from candidates. Your team is also a great resource for common challenges new hires encounter. Whether there is a project on the talent acquisition team or not, keep this line of communication and feedback open and help them continuously improve their hiring process.

3. **If focus groups are being created to address the largest concerns in annual engagement survey results, participate.** Have multiple people from your team be a part of these groups to facilitate the discussion because they're skilled in this. Your team interacts with every single person in the organization, and it makes sense for you to understand employee sentiments to improve. From there, you can help create a project plan and identify next steps.

4. **Attend individual team meetings and begin to form trusting relationships.** Be curious and ask questions, but be respectful and don't distract from the agenda. Standalone meetings with your stakeholders are great, but nothing beats firsthand feedback from employees who are doing the work.

When your team is ingrained into the business's major operations, the business can't move forward without you. Everboarding is your way of making your team crucial for business success. You become indispensable.

Share Your Vision

To effectively implement an everboarding strategy, you have to stop looking at it as a linear experience. It is not an "if this, then that" scenario. Everboarding is a collection of experiences that aligns with the individual journey that new hires will take at your organization. Before they can navigate their learning independently, however, you must provide structure and clarity through the application of three thoughtful phases. This will require buy-in, support, and participation from the key players in a new-hire's journey—particularly managers and stakeholders.

First, how involved are the managers and your talent development team in onboarding new hires? Which of these most aligns with your organization's current state?

1. Managers make an appearance on day one and don't see their new employee again until they graduate from training.
2. Managers start one-on-ones in the first week and call their new employee daily. The training team provides minimal formal training.
3. Training is delivered by the training team and performance conversations pick up with their manager afterward.

If you chose number 1, then this chapter is for you. If you answered number 2, then this chapter is also for you. If you answered number 3, this chapter is still for you. An everboarding strategy is unique to your organization because it's completely customizable no matter how engaged the key players are right now.

Now, here are some steps you can take to gain alignment from your organizational leaders:

1. **Get buy-in.** Building trust and credibility takes time. Start by asking for it! Interview the executive and seek to understand their perspective of what good and finished looks like.

2. **Get participation.** This comes from belief in your process and resources. Once the interview is over, establish a monthly review session with your executive steering committee (ESC) to maintain alignment. Use this time to solicit feedback on your efforts as they evolve.
3. **Get support.** Strive to get commitment and connection to the value you're creating. Consider establishing ground rules that require a leader's attendance to certain meetings and events. This keeps them interested and engaged in the work you're doing.

Once you've achieved support, you can begin to take action on implementing everboarding's three phases (Figure 1-1).

Figure 1-1.
Everboarding Chunked Out

An employee's experience from being a new hire to self-directing their growth is similar to eating dinner at a restaurant you've never been to. Your server greets you and gets your individual order, you substitute with your preferences, the chef makes accommodations and prepares your food, and then your server brings it to you to enjoy. The plate comes out with a thoughtful arrangement, and you have little to no knowledge of the chaos and obstacles that may have occurred in the kitchen to get the finished dish in front of you.

Much like everboarding, an employee's experience is unique to their preferences, needs, and selection. The meal you ate was from a list of choices and it was adjusted for you; similarly, your talent development team will guide employees to the next piece of learning they need to consume. It's like I always tell my managers, "They don't need to know how the sausage is cooked. We just need to provide a fully cooked one, and then send them off with leftovers for tomorrow when they forget what it tastes like." In other words, this should feel fluid to new hires even if you and their managers are chunking it out behind the scenes.

In this scenario, you and your talent development team are the chefs and the manager is the server; you're all working together to guide the learner through each phase.

Onboarding

I hear a lot of buzz about everboarding picking up X number of days after onboarding. However, I don't agree with the idea because your onboarding program is unique to your organization. As a consultant, I have worked with organizations of all sizes in many different industries, and I can say with certainty that no one is onboarding for a set amount of time across the board, even in the same industry. The truth is, there is no magic number of days, and there's no way of knowing exactly when your new hire will need more reinforcement.

Formal onboarding still has a place in employee development because it is the most crucial phase new employees will go through. If you get onboarding wrong, the rest becomes irrelevant extra work because first impressions affect future engagement. Think of onboarding as your "show." You're the director and you call the shots. Your new hire is too new to know what they don't know at your organization, which means it's up to you to guide them. Training and talent development is here to ensure new employees are set up for success with a strong foundation.

There will come a time when the manager must step up to the plate for their newest employee—that's the development phase—but with an everboarding approach, that manager will inherit an employee who has already established good habits, confidence, and a learning-first attitude.

Because I get asked, "How long should onboarding last?" so often, it's worth unpacking some. Consider these two questions:

1. When is a new hire considered fully ramped in their role? (Use one type of role.)
2. When do you graduate a new hire? Or, how long is your current onboarding program?

Are your answers the same or are they different? More often than not, the learning and training ends before the employee is performing independently. Everboarding supports your new hire up to and beyond their independence. The first phase of everboarding ends once formal training drops below 40 percent each week, meaning, they're spending more time learning on the job than learning outside the job. Moving from the onboarding phase to the development phase requires a smooth handoff between the training team and the manager.

When I was a part of a large healthcare staffing company, our onboarding program was a well-oiled machine. The handoff to the manager was quite simple—they picked up where we left off. In the first eight weeks, a member of the training team coached the new hire with scheduled weekly one-on-ones, and the manager was required to attend. In those one-on-ones, we reviewed the employee's weekly performance metrics, discussed how they were acclimating to our technology and their team, and went over any assessments they took. We believed that this was the best way to ensure continuity and help the managers understand how to meet their employees where they were.

Through the onboarding phase of your everboarding strategy, you will establish support teams to directly and indirectly guide your new employees through their initial training. This includes a success team made up of you (or someone on your team), the employee's manager, and a performance-focused mentor. You will also shift away from one-size-fits-all onboarding to a more personalized experience. And you will swap out graduations for milestone celebrations, which reinforce that an employee's development does not stop once onboarding ends—it continues through the development phase with their manager to the refinement phase where they're leading their own continuous growth.

Development

This book offers a behind-the-scenes look at an everboarding approach to employee development. And while it's not meant to be shared with a new hire, they must understand what performance expectations will change and shift once a member of the training team is not meeting with them frequently.

It seems obvious right? You'll create a library of on-demand content for employees to access whenever they want. Then, you'll provide managers with assessments, track them in your learning management system (LMS) or other performance management tool, and measure effectiveness over time. If only it were that easy.

More than likely, employees will not make time for learning unless it leads to a promotion, money, or praise; or worse, if they're on a performance improvement plan (PIP) and are desperate to turn it around. On the other hand, managers will likely demonstrate unconscious bias, assess differently, and, unfortunately, feel like your L&D efforts have become yet another box to check on their long list of tasks.

Manager-led employee development is only effective if the manager is equipped to coach, assess, and steer the employee toward the available resources. When managers feel prepared and supported, they can be more confident in their interactions with employees and more willing to apply and adhere to your vision.

Selecting a universal coaching or performance management model is one way to support managers. Without one, you leave a lot to chance because leaders across the organization will be speaking a different language, causing disruption, confusion, and delayed performance. In chapter 8, we'll dive into manager enablement. For now, let's focus on alignment of outcomes.

Once the development phase is in action, take time to create a playbook for your managers. This playbook includes what new hires learn and when, what they will be assessed on and how, and guidance for managers around how to assess their new employee during this phase.

An alignment meeting with your managers can help provide clarity around the contributions and responsibilities of each group. Table 1-1 is an example of how I've partnered with managers in the past to establish important components of a new hire's learning journey.

Table 1-1.
Example of Partnership Between the Training Team and Managers in the Development Phase

Modes	Drivers	Mechanics
Milestone skill assessments	Weeks 3, 9, and 16 scheduled assessments	• Led by manager, supported by the training team • Employee and manager evaluations • Rubric provided for ongoing measurement
Skill alignment	Team and individual key performance indicators (KPIs)	• The assessments are flexible • Assessments align with current and future expectations • Created with collaboration
Training check-ins	60- and 90-day scheduled check-ins	• Ensure smooth transition • Continued support with conversations and survey • Needs analysis

During the development phase, even though the manager is heavily involved, it is still your duty to provide the milestone assessments and determine when they need to happen. Otherwise, they won't get done. Managers are very busy, and milestone assessments won't be a priority, especially if they think the new hire is on track in their skill and competency development. Feedback needs to be provided within the new hire's workflow so they stay the course.

Schedule the alignment meeting before you get too far into the design of this phase. That way, you give everyone a chance to connect team goals and training goals and to identify roadblocks and risk factors. Here are some tips to facilitate the alignment conversation:
1. Capture the goals of each individual team within the company and document them.
2. Identify the potential roadblocks that come with implementing a new technology and how you will overcome them.
3. Consider these scenarios:
    - Who has the capacity to assess each new hire? Is it only the manager?
    - If that person leaves tomorrow, is someone else prepared to manage the assessment?
    - Do you anticipate any changes affecting the training and performance assessments or the skills needed for the role?
    - Is there a place to track progress and ensure information is up to date?
    - What resources do you need to secure (as well as roles and responsibilities) to keep this process sustainable?

These questions and more will help you create your own alignment plan to power the development phase of everboarding. Do not skip this step. It will serve you well later to slow down, ask the right questions, and gain agreement before launching it.

Refinement

The last phase, refinement, is only effective after you've established a strong partnership between the training team and the manager. You should now have an employee who solicits feedback, knows how to learn at work, and has an awareness of what they don't know. As a bonus, their growth will continue as they take on mentorship roles.

A great refinement program is not content-centric. I fully support the creation and promotion of a robust content library. Having learning content available and accessible at work or at home is essential for maintaining an engaged workforce and cultivating a learning culture. When we consider what self-led learning means, we often envision on-demand learning that lives in our LMS, learning experience platform (LXP), or content management system (CMS). But, what if self-led learning went beyond LMS-powered courses?

Self-led learning requires you to create opportunities that are relevant to the learner's individual needs and goals. For example, in a past role, I was getting feedback from the vice president of sales that the account executives (pre-sales) and the account manager (post-sales) were in constant conflict. They tried remedying the disagreements on a case-by-case basis. The most common source of conflict was the account executive overpromising the customer deliverables that the account manager was inheriting. Oftentimes, this resulted in a churned customer, and fingers were pointed in both directions.

This inspired an opportunity for employees across the organization to try a role for a day. It required a lot of preparation to pull off, but the return on investment was worth it. The account executive and account manager switched roles for a day, and then another day, and another. After three days of walking in one another's shoes, they both gained empathy. We could have simply pulled them into a room, built an LMS course, or continued with our case-by-case resolution, but the role reversal proved more effective. After all, we learn more by doing than by listening.

Creating reinforcement opportunities can take many forms, and it certainly takes time. In Table 1-2, you'll find a high-level overview of a reinforcement strategy that provides ongoing development for employees who have finished their initial onboarding.

The most effective way to continue supporting an employee past the development phase is by blending a variety of learning retention methods. When designing self-led learning experiences, you still need to support their retention. The best method is combining multiple forms versus choosing only one. In Figure 1-2, you'll find common methods used by instructional designers to increase knowledge transfer and application.

Table 1-2.
Example of a Reinforcement Strategy During the Refinement Phase

Modes	Drivers	Mechanics
Self-paced content	Product or service content library	• Beyond initial product or service training (e.g., course levels 201, 202, and 203) • Accessed by employee • Agile to fit their development needs
Performance tracking	Individual competency development	• Manager has bird's-eye view • Progress and efforts are connected
Monthly training	• Skills (personal) • Refreshers • Skills (professional) • Industry	• Product and industry updates • Product marketing, vendors, and key leaders • Optional durable skills training

Figure 1-2.
Common Learning Retention Methods

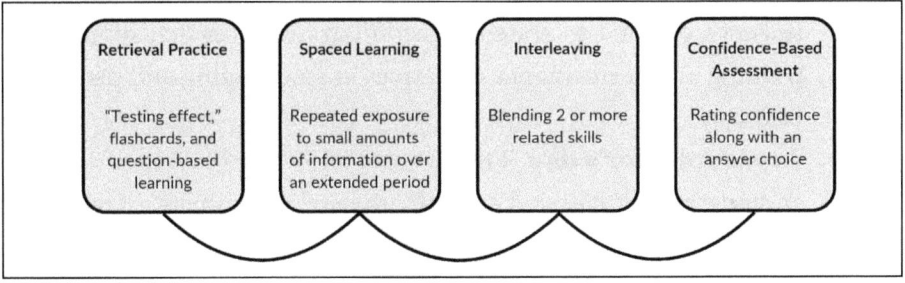

Stepping out of an LMS course and creating real-world experiences doesn't have to be a daunting task. When you're a small team or a team of one, and resources such as time are limited, you can lean on these concepts to make a big impact with little effort:

- **Knowledge checks.** Use these to drive individual awareness instead of evaluating competency. Some learning events should be a safe environment to practice, fail, and recover without consequences or feedback.
- **Gap training.** Use technology that's already in place to identify gap training needs. Conversation intelligence tools, internal

ticketing systems, and content management systems all provide valuable data.
- **Office hours.** Help promote open communication, foster teamwork, and ensure that individuals have an opportunity to connect with the relevant people within the organization.
- **Job shadowing.** This can be used to provide a realistic preview of the work environment, culture, and dynamics of a different team or role.
- **Mentoring for emerging leaders.** Match mentors and mentees based on their compatibility, areas of expertise, and the developmental needs of emerging leaders.
- **Podcasts.** Topics can include leadership skills, industry trends, internal tech stack, durable skills, and more. Podcasts allow employees to explore different areas of interest so they don't have to leave the organization for the knowledge.
- **Learning playlist.** This can serve as a road map or guide for learners, offering a curated collection of resources that support training and performance objectives in an engaging and personalized way.
- **Trade roles for a day.** This strategy allows employees to gain an understanding of and empathy toward a teammate's day-to-day activities.
- **Collaboration channels.** Use Teams or Slack to create niche channels for discussion, knowledge sharing, and FAQ identification. Channel topics could be anything such as competitors, objections, or tools.
- **Curator.** If you're fortunate to have the people resources to have a curator, prioritize them! Using a curator is a great way to capture legacy knowledge, ensure transfer across the organization, and make it consumable.

Overall, these resources are flexible and can be tailored to fit your organization's vision and current practices. Learners can engage with each of these at their own pace and feel a sense of accomplishment. Accessibility is your secret weapon to making the reinforcement phase a success.

Establish a Clear Charter for Alignment

It is paramount to the success and growth of any organization to establish a clear and comprehensive charter for training and employee development programs that delineates the responsibilities of the talent development team and the managers you support. A charter is a guiding framework that ensures seamless coordination, efficient use of resources, and, most importantly, the development of employees with an everboarding strategy.

The talent development team is primarily responsible for onboarding new hires and providing them with the fundamental skills and knowledge required to excel in their roles. This includes introducing them to company policies, procedures, and basic job training. The talent development team can offer expertise in instructional design and delivery, assisting managers in implementing effective development plans for their teams.

Meanwhile, managers are tasked with the ongoing development of their direct reports, focusing on role-specific skills enhancement and fostering team assimilation. Managers can provide invaluable insights into the specific skill sets and competencies required for success on their teams. They can also help the talent development team tailor programs to meet these needs most effectively.

By clearly delineating these responsibilities, the charter eliminates ambiguity and ensures that neither party oversteps its bounds, leading to a more streamlined and effective training process. This collaboration ensures that talent initiatives are aligned with the strategic objectives of the organization and the developmental needs of individual employees and teams, maximizing their impact and value.

Your charter can set clear expectations for the talent development team and managers, holding everyone accountable for the successful onboarding and development of employees. By defining the metrics and benchmarks outlined in the charter, you can measure progress, identify deficiencies, and implement corrective actions promptly. This accountability fosters your everboarding strategy because it ensures training initiatives and managerial support are constantly refined to better meet the evolving needs of the organization and its employees.

Your charter can also help you promote consistency and standardization across the organization. By outlining standardized processes and procedures for onboarding, manager involvement, and ongoing development, the charter ensures that all employees receive a uniform, high-quality training experience, regardless of their role or department. This consistency not only enriches and expands the efficiency of onboarding and ongoing development, but also reinforces organizational values of transparency and inclusivity.

Table 1-3 offers an example talent development team charter. Here's a list of what to include:

Mission statement:
- *Purpose and scope.* Provide a brief introduction defining the charter's purpose and scope, including the types of training covered (such as onboarding, manager coaching, or ongoing development) and the target audience (such as new hires, existing employees, or managers).

Training department responsibilities:
- *Onboarding.* Clearly outline the training department's responsibilities for welcoming new hires; introducing them to company policies, culture, and values; and providing initial orientation.
- *Basic job training.* Specify the training department's role in delivering the foundational knowledge and skills required for employees to perform their roles effectively, including technical skills, job-specific tasks, and compliance training.
- *Ongoing training program development.* Detail the training department's responsibility for designing, developing, and delivering training programs, ensuring they are relevant, engaging, and aligned with organizational objectives.
- *Evaluation and feedback.* Define processes for assessing the effectiveness of training programs, collecting feedback from

participants, and making necessary adjustments to improve future programs.
- *Performance.* Define the training department's role in assessing, guiding, and tracking employee performance.

People manager responsibilities:
- *Ongoing development.* Clearly outline managers' responsibilities for supporting the ongoing development of their team members, including identifying skills gaps, providing role-specific training and coaching, and facilitating career growth opportunities.
- *Team assimilation.* Specify managers' roles in integrating new hires into their teams, fostering a supportive and inclusive work environment, and promoting collaboration and teamwork.
- *Performance science.* Define managers' responsibilities for setting performance expectations, providing regular feedback, and supporting employee growth and development through performance evaluations and goal setting.
- *Collaboration and communication.* Establish channels for communication and collaboration between the training department and managers, facilitating the exchange of information, feedback, and best practices. Schedule regular meetings or check-ins to discuss training needs, progress, and any challenges or opportunities for improvement.

Additional components:
- *Metrics and evaluation.* Define key performance indicators (KPIs) and metrics for assessing the effectiveness of training initiatives and the impact on employee performance and organizational goals. Specify processes for collecting, analyzing, and reporting training data, including participant feedback, performance metrics, and training program evaluations.
- *Quality assurance.* Implement quality assurance processes to maintain the integrity and effectiveness of your training programs, including regular audits, reviews, and updates to training materials and processes. Consider including a content

governance strategy with representation from each team or department that your team supports.
- *Roles and responsibilities matrix.* Provide a clear matrix or table summarizing the roles and responsibilities of the training department and managers at each stage of the training process, from onboarding to ongoing development.
- *Approval and review process.* Keep it agile! Outline procedures for approving and updating the charter, including designated stakeholders responsible for review and approval. Establish a timeline or schedule for reviews and revisions to ensure the charter remains current and relevant to evolving organizational needs.

Table 1-3.
Example Talent Development Team Charter

Mission Statement	To empower employees at all levels to achieve their full potential through innovative learning experiences, continuous development opportunities, and strategic alignment with organizational goals.
Goals	• Equip employees with the skills, knowledge, and behaviors needed to drive business success. • Align talent development initiatives with organizational strategies to support scalability and long-term growth. • Enhance employee engagement and retention by providing meaningful development opportunities.
Scope and Supporting Tactics	The talent development team is responsible for designing, delivering, and managing all programs related to employee onboarding, learning, development, and leadership readiness. This includes new-hire orientation, professional skill building, performance enablement, and succession planning.
Stakeholders	• Receivers: employees • Supporters: senior leaders and hiring managers
Key Deliverables	Next 6 months: • Metrics dashboards for tracking learning participation, engagement, and outcomes • Quarterly updates to leadership on talent development progress and impact • Succession planning tools and talent pipeline reports

Table 1-3. *(continued)*

	6–18 months: • Comprehensive onboarding and everboarding programs • Customized learning pathways for specific roles, departments, and career levels • Leverage current technology investments for assessments and specialized training programs	
Metrics	• Leading: engagement, time-to-proficiency, and manager involvement • Lagging: performance metrics, retention, and employee engagement scores	
Talent Development and Leadership Alignment		
	What role does the TD team play?	What role does leadership play?
Content Development	Ownership of the ADDIE process	Subject matter expertise, need identification, and evaluation
Content Deployment	Onboarding, certifications, and product updates in the LMS	Support completion and participation
Training	Facilitation and assessment	Support completion and participation
Coaching	Role plays, group discussion, and assessment feedback	Day-to-day, performance reviews, and training reinforcement
Employee Feedback	Formal surveys at key tenure points	Casual, first-hand feedback shared with the talent development team for improvement

The establishment of your charter is instrumental for fostering the growth, development, and performance of both employees and your organization as a whole. By clearly defining roles and responsibilities, promoting accountability and collaboration, and ensuring consistency and standardization, your charter provides a guiding framework that empowers your team and managers to be more effective. This helps you nurture talent, drive performance, and achieve business objectives long after the onboarding phase.

Learning That You Can Scale

In this chapter, we debunked the myth that everboarding is merely a continuation of onboarding. Instead, everboarding fosters a culture of growth, integrating learning initiatives with talent management practices like performance management. The result is an environment where success is measured by progress and improvement, not just a willingness to learn.

Effective everboarding requires active involvement from talent development teams as partners, allies, and guides for managers and leaders. It is not a formal program but an ongoing effort to maintain conversations, collaboration, and alignment across teams. This chapter provides actionable steps to integrate your team into major business operations, becoming indispensable to the organization's success.

Onboarding is linear, but everboarding isn't. Think of it as a collection of personalized experiences that evolve along with the employee's journey. By gaining buy-in, participation, and support from organizational leaders, you can align efforts to implement the three phases of everboarding.

The onboarding phase remains foundational, setting the tone for an employee's growth. Through thoughtful design and seamless handoffs to managers, new hires develop confidence, good habits, and a learning-first attitude to enhance performance. The development phase builds on this foundation, shifting ownership to the manager and focusing on performance and continuous improvement. Finally, the refinement phase empowers employees to take charge of their growth while remaining supported by talent management systems.

Everboarding is more than just a strategy; it's a transformation of how organizations view and support employee development, ensuring every individual has the tools and opportunities to thrive beyond their first few weeks on the job.

Part 1
Training-Led Onboarding

CHAPTER 2
Establishing Support Systems

Everboarding Myth #2
It's too expensive and resource intensive.

It's much easier than you might think to put yourself in a new hire's shoes. Think about it: You've been welcomed into an organization as a new hire. If you recall, no onboarding experience was ever the same as another. For me, there were times when I was simply ushered through HR paperwork, shown a quick video overview, and left to fend for myself; other times, I had engaging conversations about the company's mission, connected with supportive teammates, and felt genuinely welcomed into the organizational culture.

The difference between those two scenarios cannot be overstated when it comes to helping employees start off on the right foot in a new role. As a learning leader, potential teammate, and colleague, you have the power to shape that crucial first impression in a way that fosters purpose, connection, and opportunity for all employees.

It's more than just checking boxes—it's about taking the time to explain the reasons behind the work, facilitating dialogue that links individual roles to organizational goals, and creating a sense of community where new hires feel empowered to grow. When you prioritize engagement over passive onboarding, you align people's energy and motivation with the company's mission from day one.

When you connect new hires with and have them developed by the right people from day one, you ensure their early days are filled with that kind of intentional onboarding experience—one in which they don't just feel like another hire, but their potential is unlocked by being welcomed into a culture of collaboration, growth, and shared purpose. By setting that tone, you, along with their colleagues and leaders, can inspire the newest employees to embrace their future with enthusiasm instead of apathy.

This chapter focuses on the critical elements of an effective support system and debunks the myth that building such a system is too expensive or resource intensive. We'll explore how leveraging the right people and tools can create a scalable model that serves both your new hires and the broader organization. By combining the success team model and a learning advisory board (LAB), we'll demonstrate that establishing support systems isn't a costly luxury—it's a strategic investment in your workforce's potential. By the end of this chapter, you'll see that as long as you have the right structure, everboarding doesn't have to drain your annual budget.

Success Team

"What makes an onboarding program successful?" I can't tell you how many times I get asked this question. It's very vague and prompts more follow-up questions, but I find myself giving the same answer: "The people are what makes your onboarding program successful—not the content, the technology, or the assessments." When you take a systems approach with people at the helm, you create everlasting results and lay the groundwork for an effective everboarding strategy.

My clients often come to me with loads of content and an existing onboarding program that is struggling. Most are extremely focused on learners' consumption and comprehension of the content. When we shift the focus to the players involved in the onboarding program, we remove the barriers affecting the new hire.

Every onboarding program that you want to sustain and scale needs a success team. For that new hire to grow and gain autonomy, they need their support team to be in alignment.

What Is a Success Team?

A success team consists of three key roles: the talent development team, the employee's manager, and a performance-focused mentor. These roles work together to create a supportive experience from day one, which leads to long-term success.

1. **The talent development team ensures consistency.** Every new hire comes in with a blank slate and is given the same content, assessments, and overall experience to succeed. The talent development team ensures that milestones are tracked and met and identifies when intervention is needed. They can also serve as field coaches to further reinforce new knowledge and skill application.
2. **The employee's manager must participate in any onboarding experience because ultimately the new hire's success falls on their shoulders.** They are there to coach, redirect, and set clear expectations for the role.
3. **The mentor is the reinforcer.** In partnership with the talent development team and the manager, the mentor ensures the new hire stays on track. They understand this new hire's job in and out because they are often in the same role. This also ensures feedback is streamlined and not solicited from other team members who don't understand their performance and progression. Additionally, this performance-focused mentor frees up the amount of time managers spend in new-hire development. This is a team effort and managers need as much support as the new employee. (Exception: If this is a new role for the organization, the mentor must be someone who directly interacts with the employee and can relate to and understand the influence their role will have on the success of the team or organization. For example, a company hires its first invoicing specialist and assigns an accounts payable clerk as their mentor.)

The success team must have a place to communicate with one another outside face-to-face interactions. Anything from a shared Google drive to formal performance software will work. The objective is to create the space for asynchronous work so barriers such as time won't get in the way of communicating.

Table 2-1 offers a quick overview of the success team's responsibilities, cadence for interaction with the new hire, and how to escalate concerns.

Table 2-1.
The Everboarding Success Team for New Hires

Who	Responsibilities	Cadence for Interaction	Escalation
Talent development team member	Ensure comprehension, administer formal assessments, and conduct formal training.	Every day until the new hire has mild autonomy	Bring concerns to the manager and make the mentor aware.
Manager	Ensure new hire is adhering to company standards and expectations, encourage their development, and provide feedback on the job.	Every day	Share concerns and feedback conversations with the talent development team and mentor.
Mentor	Engage in scenario-based coaching and be a go-to resource.	Once a week (formally) but may interact more if solicited by new hire	Bring concerns to the manager but keep the talent development team informed. All formal mentoring sessions are documented in writing.

Your new hires need a well-coordinated success team to build a foundation of support and success, and your everboarding strategy requires a similar structure at the organizational level. While the success team focuses on the new hire's immediate experience, the broader framework for sustaining and scaling your onboarding and everboarding programs depends on collaboration and alignment across the organization.

This is where a learning advisory board comes into play.

Learning Advisory Board

Have you ever accomplished anything alone? Probably not. Even Olympic athletes competing in individual events have a team of people behind them. Your talent strategy is no exception. You need a team of people that goes well beyond the TD team to infuse it into the organization and keep your efforts relevant and everlasting. You need a learning advisory board (LAB) to help hone the content (we'll delve into aligning with key business partners later).

I have been a team of one more than once, and truthfully, I was overwhelmed. I have also been overwhelmed while on a team of 20. The amount of work a talent development team can tackle is limited but never-ending. Your team can lean on subject matter experts and divide and conquer, but without a strategy for maintenance, the work isn't scalable.

So, what can you do? Extend the expertise and the involvement outside your team. I was at a startup technology company when I took on a role that had me supporting the entire organization. I tried to do what I had always done: Get the information I needed from the subject matter expert, build the course, assign it, revisit it, and then put it into my cycle for revisiting it for a refresh. My team went from zero courses when I walked in the door to more than 100 in 90 days. At that rate, I had no time to review my work and keep it relevant. I decided I needed ownership over content for each team, but lacked the budget to add headcount to my team.

It became evident that I needed to teach my craft to members of each team—marketing, sales, product, customer success, customer service, and operations—who could then review content for their respective audience. Creators from the teams already existed, but I was spinning my wheels trying to make the course engaging for learners and ensuring the information was accurate and up to date. Most of what my LAB at that startup did was remove biases and confusing information, but they also met with me monthly to provide feedback. Our goal was to keep learning relevant and address the current needs of their teams.

The LAB provided firsthand feedback into my top questions around my efforts:
1. What is most important to that specific team?
2. What should we start, stop, and continue doing with our courses?
3. Is the content adding value to their work?

The final evaluation for the LAB's effectiveness was a crucial question: How do you know the value of your learning services at your organization? (If you walk away with anything in this section, it should be this.)

To make your onboarding program and everboarding strategy work, you must know the answer to this scenario: *When an employee is stuck and can't move forward with a task, where do they turn?* Is it a person, like their manager? Or are they going right to the content you create? If it's not the latter, your content is not valuable to them. They have to find it relevant and crucial in their time of need. If it's not, your services are dispensable and you're no longer in the business of learning at your organization.

Find a way to be the resource new hires turn to in a moment of need. Until then, you are only checking a box for initial comprehension. Beyond that, they are performing without you and likely overwhelming their manager with questions. Lean on your LAB to help you reach that point of influence.

In my experience, the best way to get LAB members on the same page is to create a charter that includes the following items (Figure 2-1):

- **Statement of purpose** defines the overarching mission of the LAB. It serves as a unifying guideline and aligns all contributors on why the LAB exists and how it ensures the quality and effectiveness of learning content. All stakeholders must understand the LAB's goals and how their roles contribute to maintaining a scalable and effective learning strategy.
- **Admin responsibilities** outline the administrative roles and duties within the LAB. By assigning departmental admins, you create a clear chain of responsibility for content creation, quality assurance, tagging, and communication across teams. This

ensures a systematic approach to content development, prevents duplication of effort, and fosters cross-departmental collaboration for relevant and scalable training.
- **Clearly defined roles for creating courses** (such as admin, manager, creator, and learner) ensure accountability at each stage of the course creation process. This structure helps streamline the workflow, maintain high-quality standards, and enable periodic reviews for content relevance. Content governance is not limited to the L&D team. You can ensure that courses are continually updated and aligned with employee development needs.
- **Branding guidelines for courses** promote consistency in the look, feel, and tone of all learning content. This helps reinforce organizational identity and professionalism in training materials. By standardizing elements—such as cover images, voice, quizzing standards, and visual styles—employees can navigate content more intuitively and feel a stronger connection to the material.
    - **An element library** provides a repository of preapproved assets (such as cover and background images and standardized sections) that streamline course creation. By working efficiently while maintaining consistency, the LAB will be able to scale its efforts without compromising quality.
    - **Lesson creation templates** help you maintain a repeatable and efficient process for building courses. Templates reduce ambiguity for creators and admins by providing a table of contents, a standardized vocabulary list, and clear stylistic dos and don'ts.
    - **A style guide** outlines specific design and pedagogical expectations to ensure every lesson aligns with organizational values and performance goals. It specifies tone, quizzing best practices, use of multimedia, and application exercises so courses are not just engaging but also effective and actionable.

Figure 2-1.
Example of a Learning Advisory Board Charter

Statement of Purpose
This document will serve as a guideline for how to follow the design and quality assurance (QA) process for deploying training to teams using our LMS.

Admin Responsibilities
Each department will have an admin. Content ideas and QA will be funneled through them. The admin will ensure that course design is consistent, tags are added accordingly, and content is made available to all relevant audiences. The admin decides if a course is beneficial to those beyond their department. The admin also communicates to the other teams if the collaboration on a course requires a SME.

Current Admins

Sales	Marketing	Operations	Product	Customer Success	Professional Services	Tech

Current Creators

Sales	Marketing	Operations	Product	Customer Success	Professional Services	Tech

When Creating Courses

Roles:
- **Creator.** Create content for which they're a SME. After finishing, add the tag "QA" and alert the team's admin by @mentioning them in the course builder. Courses must be revisited every 90 days for freshness and relevance.
- **Admin.** Act as QA for content for which they are the SME and create content. After reviewing content created by others, remove the "QA" tag, add new tags, add to appropriate learning groups, and publish.
- **Managers.** Review content after admin if needed.
- **Learner.** Bring ideas for courses to their department admin.

Figure 2-1. *(continued)*

Branding Within Courses

Element library:
- Cover images (specifics for teams)
- Background images
- Sections (introduction, overview, and knowledge checks)

Template for course creation:
- TOC
- List of terms to use
- Things to avoid

Style guide:
- Language and voice to be used
- Quizzing standards:
  - When to use (at the end or in the middle)
  - What to use (knowledge check, multiple choice, or multiple select)
  - How many to use per course
- Practical application (work with talent development team to create these)
- How many images and videos per course
- How many sections per course
- Embedding: Caption! Avoid using links

Building a LAB helps your content stay relevant, but even well-designed courses can miss the mark if the team isn't taking into consideration how and when learners consume the material. Content is one part of the equation—engagement and application are just as critical. As the world has shifted to hybrid and remote work, I've quickly learned that the way learners interact with training material drastically changes depending on the environment. This shift has brought a new challenge: designing learning programs that intentionally address how employees consume and engage with content in a virtual or hybrid world.

Down Time and Intention for Consumption and Engagement

Before the world went remote in 2020, I was working in a hybrid environment with a dispersed workforce. It was a big adjustment for me because

I went from training and coaching in-person five days a week to zero. My organization believed that everyone should be given the same experiences regardless of where they were located. So, whenever I facilitated a training program, I'd go into the conference room and every single person was on a laptop, even those in the room. The way I designed my learning programs had to change drastically to be successful in this hybrid environment.

When the employees are in the room with you, breaks are built in. Tenured employees go back to their desk after training ends, and new hires get breaks in onboarding to apply what they've learned on their own. If they need help, you're right there to assist. Suddenly, those days of seeing when someone was struggling were gone. And because many organizations are still operating with a remote or hybrid workforce, it's important that you consider two crucial components of hybrid learning programs: breaking up the day and making yourself available.

Breaking Up the Day

Your new employees still need breaks. They need the ability to walk away from their computer entirely and decompress. Somewhere along the way many companies copied what they were doing in-person and pasted it onto a virtual schedule, but that doesn't fly anymore. It's unrealistic to expect a new employee and a trainer to sit in a virtual classroom—or a physical classroom for that matter—for eight hours.

I have a rule that for every 90 minutes of virtual learning, new hires receive a 45-minute window to practice and another 30 minutes to do as they wish. We then review that topic before moving onto the next.

> **Pro Tip**
>
> I don't hear this being done often enough, but I find it effective to turn some of your industry knowledge, customer stories, or company-wide courses into podcast episodes. I encourage employees to walk during break time, if they're able, and these podcasts are available for them to listen to.

Making Yourself Available

How many times do you send an employee off to complete a scavenger hunt or another self-guided activity only to be told they couldn't do it? You set clear instructions, ensured they had the activity, and asked if they were comfortable finishing it solo, but it still wasn't done!

The distractions for remote workers are just as bad as the in-person ones. You can set deadlines, but ultimately it is on them to follow through. You're not their manager and the line of accountability can be blurry. I like to give the benefit of the doubt—they may have struggled with the assignment and were worried that asking for help would make it look like they weren't paying attention. You could make so many guesses, but you need to take accountability for it yourself. What can you do?

You can make yourself available. Check in with them after you've assigned an activity. Schedule a review call and include their manager on it if possible—they likely won't want their manager to know if they didn't get something done. Use this approach only for the wildly important skills they need to learn and not a course like a company orientation.

Making yourself available is also about supporting them when they're apprehensive to ask for help. Send a message through a tool like Teams or Slack to check in and ask about specific things they're working on. In their first month, ask how they're feeling about the job and the organization at least once a week. You may be surprised to find where you can assist in bridging gaps between a new hire and their manager, a process or policy, or larger organizational communications.

Protect the Wellbeing of These New Investments

Onboarding is an ideal time to establish a foundation for mental health and well-being at your organization. From benefits to organizational culture behaviors, new employees will use and mirror what they know to be true. Many employees bring prior negative employment experiences with them that you can't control, but you can put their mind at ease by making them feel supported. A comfortable employee will perform better than an anxious one.

Start by informing them about the available benefits. This was most likely shared during the interview process, but a refresher in week one will reassure them that these benefits are meant to be used.

In the onboarding phase, new hires primarily work with the talent development team and HR, so you can set the tone. Here are a few suggestions:

- Introduce mental health and well-being resources as part of the onboarding materials (including EAPs, wellness apps, or mental health days).
- Include a mental health and wellness session as part of the onboarding program. This can be led by an HR representative or an external expert.
- Share company values around mental health and well-being during orientation, emphasizing inclusion and open communication.
- Provide opportunities for new hires to anonymously share their well-being concerns or stressors as part of onboarding surveys.
- Include mindfulness workshops or guided meditation in onboarding to introduce healthy stress management techniques.

While in the development phase, new employees primarily work with their manager, so you—and the manager—need to shift to modeling mental health and well-being behaviors. You can:

- Train managers to incorporate mental health questions into regular one-on-ones, such as, "How are you managing your workload?" or "How can I support your well-being?"
- Equip managers with tools to recognize signs of burnout and have empathetic conversations about mental health.
- Align professional growth opportunities with personal well-being goals, encouraging employees to develop skills without overextending themselves.

Once the employee moves to the refinement phase, they should take ownership of their own mental health at work while receiving ongoing support from the organization. You can:

- Make mental health and work-life balance part of performance reviews and career discussions, asking questions like, "Are your goals aligned with your personal well-being?"
- Connect employees with opportunities like nonprofit board service (aligned with their other work) to develop executive presence while fostering personal fulfillment.
- Recognize employees for achieving personal milestones, like completing wellness training or advocating for mental health initiatives.

Insert Your Support System Here!

I've laid out what a success team LAB is, and the need for breaks and education on well-being at work. These are all pieces of a new hire's ongoing support system. We'll talk more about systems throughout this book, but think of this as your starting point.

In this chapter, I covered success teams before discussing LABs for a reason: You should establish your success team framework before establishing your LAB because those team members can do more good (or harm) than any content strategy ever could. Remember, the people are what makes a successful onboarding program.

People will always be the first line of defense for a new hire when they're stuck or unsure. Mentors must have the skills and capabilities to coach and guidance for their formal sessions (we'll cover mentors more in the next two chapters). Confirm managers know how their new hire is progressing and are prepared to hold their onboarding check-ins. Without structure, you create an environment of survival, which leads to confusion and regression for new employees.

Your LAB creates clarity around what's working and what isn't, and ultimately helps you articulate the value of your onboarding training programs. Know where your employees go in the moment of need. Become that resource. Your LAB will help get you there. I recommend including leaders without titles from each team. This not only provides a leadership experience for them to grow, but they also typically have more time than formal leaders do and are more connected to the work the team is doing. As always, do what's best for your organization in these scenarios because internal politics can play an important role in your choices.

You create the training schedule, so you have the power to say when new hires are working and when they are taking breaks during the onboarding program. Wield your power for good. Help them feel supported with a training schedule that is designed for the modern working world. Don't put them through a college course—they are adults being asked to perform, which requires a great deal of individual engagement and external encouragement. Remind them to take the breaks you've given them and to trust the process you've created. You designed a program with their well-being in mind, and it's important they know the reasons behind it.

Now that your onboarding support system is in place, let's turn to how you can personalize onboarding and avoid a one-size-fits-all approach.

CHAPTER 3
Making Onboarding Personal

Everboarding Myth #3
Everboarding can be a one-size-fits-all approach.

Onboarding is like a free trial at a new gym—it will determine whether someone chooses to continue showing up and putting in the work. If the foundational experience is inadequate or feels disorganized, you will immediately lose their trust and their belief in your organization will falter. Once that's gone, it is very challenging or nearly impossible to earn back. We will discuss a few strategies to get your onboarding in tip-top shape throughout this part of the book, but let's begin with making it personal.

When an employee joins an organization, they have their own set of expectations for the experience they'll have in the near and distant future. They put their trust in the employer to guide them from day one to day 500 and beyond. There is little you can assume about what those expectations are because each new hire comes with varied life experiences, professional journeys, and personal perspectives of the world around them. However, simply being aware of this is not enough. You have to design for it.

In this chapter, we'll explore how to create an onboarding experience that's as dynamic and diverse as the employees you onboard. New employees bring a unique blend of experiences and expectations. Yet, many onboarding programs fail to account for this individuality, defaulting to a one-size-fits-all approach that leaves some employees disengaged from day one.

To truly make onboarding personal, you must design it intentionally, tailoring the experience to different personas, adapting schedules for varied roles, and leveraging mentors as partners in the process. Mentors aren't just guides—they're critical to early development and long-term success. But their influence depends on proper preparation and active involvement. (Due to the importance of mentors, we'll tackle them separately in the next chapter.)

Employee Personas

I suggest identifying the employee personas that make up your organization before you tackle any other part of this chapter. An *employee persona* is a profile of your audience that you'll use in all stages of employee development, not just during onboarding. (This may sound familiar especially if you've spent any time in sales or marketing because it is similar to a buyer persona.) Knowing your workforce's personas gives your team credibility and helps you gain buy-in for ongoing participation in an organization with an everboarding strategy.

An employee persona's profile includes characteristics like demographics, education level, technical skills, professional background, and even hobbies and past experiences with learning at work. The size of your organization and hiring goals will affect how many personas you need. I encourage you to think about it at the business function level, such as engineering, sales, customer service, and IT. Each of these groups will have diverse characteristics, making it too hard to narrow down only one persona to design for.

Building a persona is not overly complex, but it does take time to collect the data you need (Figure 3-1). Your technology stack will play a huge part in this collection. Use your human resources information system (HRIS), LMS, or LXP to gather quantitative data. For qualitative data, you can use a survey tool, but don't discount the value of first-hand interviews; that conversational type of data gathering will make these results even more powerful. Sit down with HR, managers, and a few employees in the group you're designing for to get insights that a survey can't provide.

Figure 3-1.
Process for Using Employee Personas

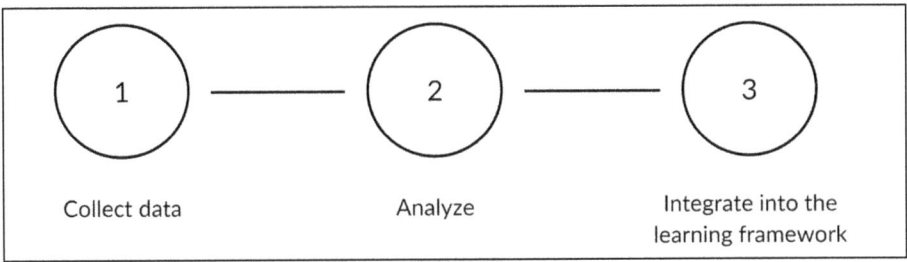

Analyze what you've collected with care. Identify any outliers and document trends you see so your persona can begin to take shape. Remember, you can't be everything to every person you survey, but you are drastically improving the experience they get from any off-the-shelf, designed-for-the-masses content they typically consume.

Now, give your persona a name and keep the conversations around program strategy and course design employee-centric. Giving the persona a name, a photo, and a description of their characteristics allows them come to life so you're no longer talking about a broad group of people (Figure 3-2). You'll be able to take a more empathetic approach to their needs once you've narrowed it down to one person to make decisions around.

Creating employee personas is just the first step. What truly matters is how you use them to design and deliver meaningful everboarding experiences. Once you've developed your personas, you can:

- **Tailor learning content to persona needs.** Use the persona profiles to customize learning materials. For example, if a persona like Luna (shown in Figure 3-2) needs mobile-friendly and bite-sized content due to the nature of how she performs her job, ensure your onboarding modules or development programs align with those preferences. Personas should guide the content's format, depth, and delivery.

- **Guide onboarding and development strategies.** Think of personas as a filter for decision making. When building onboarding schedules or development programs, ask, "Would this approach meet the needs and motivations of [*persona's name*]?" From flexible scheduling to self-paced learning, your development initiatives need to resonate with each persona's goals and challenges.
- **Empower mentors and managers.** Share the personas with the mentors and managers involved in the onboarding process. These profiles will help them better understand the individuals they are supporting and give them insights into how to connect, motivate, and coach effectively. For instance, Luna's manager can emphasize practical, career-oriented learning opportunities that directly tie to her goals.
- **Evaluate and refine programs.** Use personas as benchmarks to evaluate your everboarding programs. Are the challenges your personas face being addressed? Are their learning goals being met? Gather feedback from employees that match these personas to assess whether your programs are hitting the mark or need further refinement.
- **Foster empathy and inclusion.** Personas bring your learners to life, shifting the conversation from "What works for most employees?" to "What works for Luna (or any other persona)?" This shift drives empathy and ensures your onboarding programs feel personal, rather than generic. It also ensures that employees feel seen and valued as individuals, fostering a sense of belonging from day one.

Pro Tip

Share the completed employee persona profile with every individual involved in employee learning, including your subject matter experts.

Figure 3-2.
Example of an Employee Persona

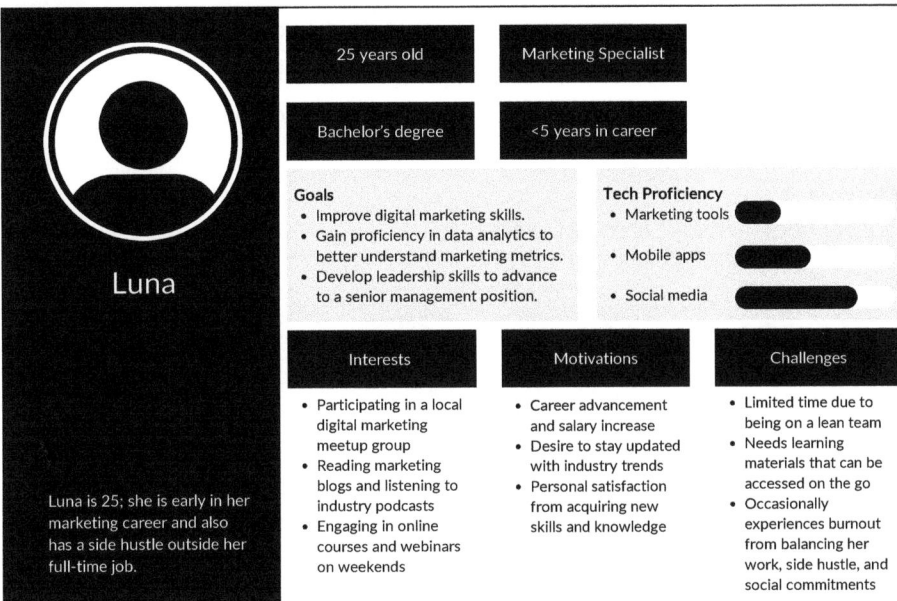

Personas aren't static. They must evolve as your workforce changes. Periodically revisit and update them to reflect new data, insights, and trends in your organization. Designing with personas in mind creates a foundation for onboarding and development that's personal and meaningful and avoids a one-size-fits-all approach without maxing out the team's stamina.

One Size Does Not Fit All

Stop creating onboarding for the masses! Once you've developed your employee personas and determined the employee life cycle, it's time to apply this knowledge to each role and create role-specific training. Tailoring the onboarding phase to each role is crucial to long-term success. The time invested is greater, but so is the ROI, which is your biggest asset in stakeholder support.

As learning and talent development leaders, we must align our efforts with business needs instead of focusing entirely on our learners' needs. The reality is that learning won't always be fun. More importantly, it needs to be crucial, consumable, and connected to a goal (Figure 3-3):

- **Crucial**—essential to the business or the role
- **Consumable**—simple, clear, and actionable
- **Connected**—aligned with measurable outcomes

Figure 3-3.
3Cs for Personalizing Learning Content

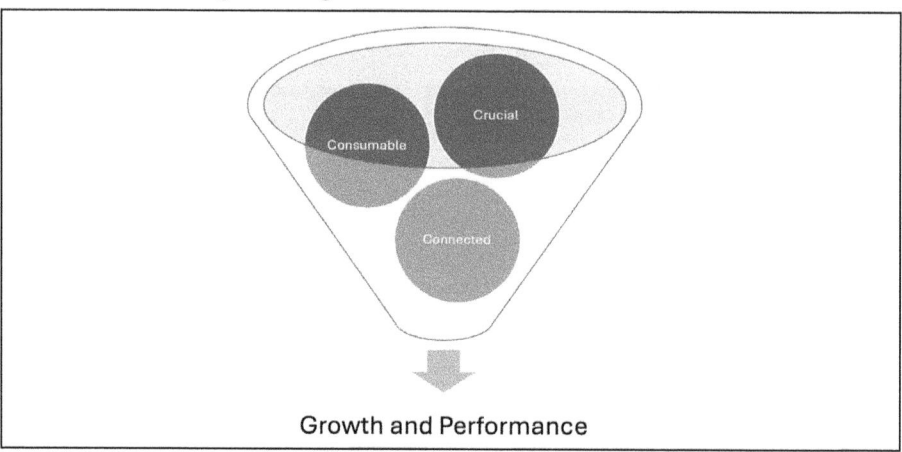

Did you see the *Top Gun* sequel, *Top Gun: Maverick*? It inspired me to launch a Top Gun–style onboarding program. It just makes sense! The idea at Top Gun is to prepare the elite, right? However, Top Gun's program is also focused on continuously sharing knowledge and skills. As each new employee joins your organization and goes through the most up-to-date, recent training program you have, they then take that knowledge back to their team. If the information isn't designed for their individual role, then there is little to share.

Follow these steps to tailor your onboarding content to a specific role:

1. **Preassess.** Identify the skills needed for the role. What challenges do you typically see when someone is hired for this position? Analyze any prehire assessment data that your talent acquisition team has collected.

2. **Establish goals.** Objectives and key results (OKRs) are ideal for tailoring training because they are focused on two vital components: clearly defined objectives and how they'll be monitored and measured. In other words, they answer the questions, "Why are you doing it and what will it take to be successful?"
3. **Identify resources.** These may include a budget for external education, people, or specific learning courses that are already available.
4. **Make the plan dynamic.** Review and update plans regularly to reflect progress, organizational changes, and any challenges that participants encounter.
5. **Celebrate.** Recognition keeps employees motivated to complete their learning experiences.

Why are we focusing on OKRs and not SMART goals? Because OKRs are more collaborative and allow you to set more ambitious goals while still being measurable. *Objectives* are simple and action-oriented and should be inspirational. They can also be long term, and a learning journey isn't a short commitment. The *key results* determine how you'll achieve the objective. You either achieve the key result or you don't. What's unique about them is they're agile and evolve over time to support the objectives.

For example, a data analyst could create this OKR:

Objective: Enhance data analysis proficiency.

Key results: Achieve proficiency in data analytics by completing two online courses or certifications in the next six months. Improve coding skills in relevant software by participating in coding bootcamp within the next nine months. Create and deliver three different projects for detailed data visualizations using Tableau and receive positive feedback from stakeholders on the clarity and effectiveness of the visual communication.

The OKR must be aligned with team and business goals. In this example, we can assume that the data analyst and their leader chose these key results because they are aligned with where the team is headed, the technology they use, and the skills that are missing.

Designing Onboarding Schedules for High-Volume Hiring Environments

If your organization has preset hire dates for the year, designing a tailored onboarding experience will be much simpler. You can predetermine which training courses can be combined and which SMEs can assist with multiple roles; then you can divide the new hires once the content becomes too specific to their individual positions. Even if you're hiring throughout the year on a more ad hoc basis, you can still benefit from planning ahead with self-led resources or conducting train-the-trainer sessions to enable multiple guest facilitators for each instructor-led course.

Consider where you can use the same resources and still add value. Just avoid the temptation to fit a course into an onboarding program if it's not directly related to the employee's core skills. For example, a sales professional would benefit from knowing how customers can submit support tickets, but they do not need to know that to begin their job. Those types of learning experiences can be applied later to give them more context around their role. Their initial weeks should focus on their primary job duties to avoid confusion and frustration.

Table 3-1 offers an example of the first week of training for two roles that have overlapping responsibilities.

Start by identifying the core knowledge and skills that every role will need, such as corporate policies, IT systems, core values, and general operational procedures. Then, set universal performance objectives, such as knowing the company's mission and vision and where to find vital internal collateral like organizational goals and objectives.

To tailor learning content to the employee's role, you have to start with assessments that identify three things:

1. Their strengths
2. Their skill level
3. Their career goals

It's essential that the learning journey is aligned with each new hire's personal goals and career aspirations. These personalized journeys are employee-owned and leader-led. Tailoring the learning content requires a collaborative approach involving both the employee and their leader, who will actively engage with one another to create, adjust, and complete the learning plan.

Table 3-1.
Example Schedules for Week 1 of Customer Service Associate and Account Manager Onboarding Programs

Day 1	Day 2	Day 3	Day 4	Day 5
Objectives				
• Core values • Mission and vision • Orientation	• Who we serve • Day in the life	• Intro to technology	• Practice scenarios	• Intro to customer interactions • Week 1 quiz
LMS Content				
• Welcome to the company • Week 1 path	• Week 1 path	• Week 1 path	• Week 1 path	• Week 1 path • Week 1 quiz
What to Review				
• Our core values • Employee benefits	• Customer reviews • Customer interviews	• Technology scavenger hunt	• Your feedback from practice	• Showing empathy
Mentor Interaction				
• Introductions	• Email or Slack check-in	• Email or Slack check-in	• Practice scenarios	• Review week 1 objectives

Benefits of Personalization

This chapter dismantled the myth that everboarding can follow a one-size-fits-all approach and emphasized the importance of personalizing onboarding experiences to reflect the unique needs and expectations of each employee. Personalization also drives empathy and inclusivity, providing a more supportive and effective learning environment. If the initial experience feels inadequate, it can undermine trust and retention. By intentionally designing onboarding programs tailored to individual roles and personas, your organization can create dynamic and inclusive experiences that foster engagement and development.

At the beginning of the chapter, I mentioned the key role that mentors play in making onboarding feel personal to new hires. Let's explore their impact more in the next chapter.

CHAPTER 4
Tapping Mentors as Your Partners in Onboarding

Everboarding Myth #4
New hires can get by with a buddy mentor during everboarding.

Mentors are not just an optional resource for onboarding. They are a critical extension. When designed thoughtfully, mentoring programs reduce the burden on SMEs and managers while providing new hires with the support they need to quickly move from fumbling to performing. Whether your organization is a small startup or a global enterprise, the right mentoring program can reduce hiring expenses and free up the manager's time.

In this chapter, we'll explore how mentoring can elevate your onboarding program and accelerate new-hire success. We'll start with the key components to your mentoring program and then cover ways to prepare mentors to take an active role in new-hire development.

Developing a New-Hire Mentoring Program

No onboarding program is ever complete without a mentoring program baked into it. You will do more work and spend more time with your SMEs without one. Think of the mentors as an extension of you and the manager. In addition to developing a peer, their role is to guide and course-correct in the absence of the training team and the hiring manager. No matter it's size—from 10 employees to 100,000—every company needs a mentoring program specific to new hires. So, let's discuss what your new-hire mentoring program needs to have and what you might need to remove.

If you have a mentoring program, it likely consists of traditional mentors, who are often more experienced individuals providing guidance and support to another person. New-hire mentoring programs are a little different because they need to support onboarding week by week with reinforcement methods. Some organizations use two types of mentors in this setting (and I'm using the word "mentor" loosely).

One type of mentor is a buddy. This person is meant to immerse the new hire into the organization's culture and answer questions that aren't specific to their role. They're simply there to put the new employee's worries and uncertainties at ease. This is similar to what schools do for new students. However, we're developing adults who come to work to perform; doing well in their job is what's most important to them.

The other type of mentor, a performance-focused mentor, is much different. They are more like coaches—focused on reducing ramp up time and taking new hires from fumbling to performing. Many new-hire mentoring programs miss the mark because they put all the job competency development on the manager. Mentors share what they know, but a coach can meet the new hire where they are and help them level up. Let's dive into how you can design a coaching program to level up your SMEs into performance-focused mentors.

Designing a performance-focused mentor program starts with conversations with a manager and their recent hires. They have valuable insights into what a new employee will do, assume, feel, and consider and can help you go even deeper into your employee personas. Managers are your allies for developing SMEs into performance-focused mentors.

When a mentor is focused on performance and helping drive results and outcomes, a new employee receives a peer coach. This should be someone who has recently been in their shoes and can identify roadblocks and make potential solutions easier. Without the mentor, reinforcement strategies for onboarding are at risk.

If you pair new hires with mentors who are too tenured, they likely won't understand what that new employee needs. Veteran employees operate with autonomy and often don't rely on best practices. In addition, mentors who are in a different role than the new hire will lack perspective and only be able to offer knowledge and understanding of another team's contribution. As a result, the new hire will likely hear the words, "I'm not sure. I'd ask your manager," over and over. Save that cross-team empathy for the performing phase of the employee journey.

Mentors Take an Active Role in Early Development

In an ideal environment, mentoring new employees is seen as a crucial added value for the organization. More often than not, I have faced opposition to pulling tenured employees away from their day to assist in developing new hires. You should expect some opposition too. When you move from using buddies to performance-focused mentors, it means asking the mentor to commit more time and attention to the new employee. Managers are often the first to stand between you and the mentor because they fear the time lost with a new commitment.

I encourage you to create a business case and focus on the value mentoring provides instead of the time commitment it requires. The total time needed from mentors is unique to your onboarding program needs. For example, I worked in an environment that allowed managers to devote time to developing their newest employees because the rest of their team had high autonomy and we weren't in a hiring spree. At another organization, however, I faced the opposite situation—managers never ate lunch and worked 60 hours a week. Few, if any, of those hours were spent developing their new employees. In the latter situation, a mentor would be leaned on more heavily, so it's important to set boundaries for engagement.

The opportunity to develop your organization's newest employees is an honor and a privilege. Mentors should feel obliged to take it seriously and put their best efforts forward. One way to generate a cultural cachet around your mentoring program is to create a job description and an application to serve (Figure 4-1). The application should require a manager's signature, prerequisites (such as tenure and performance ratings), and a formal interview with the talent development team.

Figure 4-1.
Mentor Application Form Example

Instructions
Please fill out this application to apply for the mentoring program. Ensure that you meet the prerequisites before submitting.

Prerequisites
- 6–24 months of tenure with the company
- Satisfactory performance ratings on your most recent review
- Manager's signature endorsing your application

Applicant Information
- Name:
- Employee ID:
- Department:

Manager's Endorsement
I hereby endorse this application and confirm that the applicant meets all prerequisites for the mentoring program.
- Manager's name:
- Manager's signature:
- Date:

Short Answer Questions
- Why do you want to become a mentor for new hires? *(Please describe your motivation and what you hope to achieve through this program.)*

- What skills and experiences do you believe are essential for a successful mentor? *(List and elaborate on the key skills and experiences you bring to the role.)*

- Describe a time when you successfully helped a colleague or team member. *(Provide details about the situation, your approach, and the outcome.)*

- What are some challenges you anticipate facing as a mentor, and how do you plan to overcome them? *(Identify potential challenges and outline your strategies for addressing them.)*

- How do you plan to build a strong relationship with your mentee? *(Explain your approach to building trust and rapport with new hires.)*

Figure 4-1. *(continued)*

- What are your goals for the mentoring relationship? *(Discuss what you aim to achieve for both yourself and your mentee.)*

Submission
Please submit your completed application to the talent development team via email.

Preparing Mentors

Take time to not only learn about why individuals want to mentor but to educate them on expectations. Ensure you know when they're available to mentor and avoid any upcoming vacations or major life events. Also talk about any communication expectations with your team, the new hire's manager, and the new employee.

Performance-focused mentors must be able to give feedback appropriately. Your efforts to use them will fail if they don't have the necessary skills. I have witnessed new-hire mentoring relationships need mediation because of poor feedback skills. When you can educate and assess your mentors on their abilities to give feedback, it not only helps the new hire, but it helps the mentor enhance their professional skills, which they can then apply to any difficult situation.

Feedback training is peer focused, so there's no need to delve into the more complex models out there for these purposes. I am a proponent of implementing the ideas outlined by Kim Scott in *Radical Candor*, but I haven't found it to be crucial for new-hire mentoring. Scott's approach to feedback emphasizes the importance of caring personally as well as challenging them directly to help them grow. It encourages leaders to create a culture of openness to foster growth, but a new employee may need time to develop trust or familiarity with the team culture to handle direct and sometimes tough feedback effectively. New-hire mentors helping their peers need a simpler approach to feedback that isn't overwhelming for the giver or receiver.

When creating a new-hire mentoring program, use a model that is easy for your mentors to remember and adopt. I call my model the BEST Feedback Model—because it's best for your employees!

- **Behavior.** Describe the specific behavior you observed. Example: "I noticed that during the client meeting, you presented your ideas very clearly and concisely."
- **Effect.** Explain the effect of the behavior. Example: "Your clear explanation helped the client understand the project goals better, which will help us move forward more efficiently."
- **Suggestion.** Offer a constructive suggestion for improvement or reinforcement of good behavior. Example: "Next time, it might be even more effective if you could include a brief summary at the end of your presentation to reinforce the key points."
- **Thanks.** Express appreciation for their efforts and contributions. Example: "Thank you for putting in the effort to prepare such a thorough presentation. It really made a difference."

Help your mentors prepare ahead of time if possible. It's inevitable that some situations won't allow them to prepare a strong feedback message for their new hire mentees, but you still need to equip them with the tools to be successful in their delivery. Here are the steps to deliver feedback using the BEST model:

1. **Prepare.** Before the feedback session, think through each component of the BEST model to ensure your feedback is clear and balanced.
2. **Be specific.** Focus on specific instances of behavior rather than general comments.
3. **Be timely.** Give feedback as soon as possible after the observed behavior to ensure it is relevant and fresh in the mentee's mind.
4. **Be supportive.** Use a positive and supportive tone to encourage the mentee and help them feel valued.
5. **Follow up.** After providing feedback, check in with your mentee to see how they are implementing your suggestions and offer further guidance if needed.

Faster New-Hire Development Through Performance-Focused Mentoring

This chapter discussed how performance-focused mentoring transforms onboarding into a seamless journey from uncertainty to confidence and capability. By shifting the traditional mentoring model into one centered on coaching and peer-driven development, your team can empower new hires to ramp up faster and more effectively. Mentors play a pivotal role in early-stage growth, offering targeted feedback, role-specific guidance, and ongoing reinforcement. With clear expectations and tools like the BEST Feedback Model, mentors can elevate new hires into high-performing contributors, while simultaneously enhancing their own leadership and communication skills. A successful mentoring program isn't just a value-add; it's a powerful organizational necessity for sustainable talent pipelines.

CHAPTER 5
Celebrating Milestones Over Graduations

Everboarding Myth #5
Everboarding picks up after 90 days of employment.

The world is evolving rapidly and our businesses are running as fast as they can to keep up. Your team's onboarding process is a critical phase in the employee life cycle. Traditionally, onboarding has been viewed as a finite process ending in a graduation that signifies a new hire is fully integrated and operational. However, this perspective often neglects the continuous development and engagement needed for the employee's long-term success.

Everboarding is only achieved when you focus on prioritizing milestones over graduations in onboarding (and in employee development generally), emphasizing that onboarding is just the launch phase, or leg 1 of a metaphorical relay. In this chapter, you'll learn how to focus your efforts on the importance of establishing and celebrating milestones and avoid the pitfalls of designing for early mastery. This means advocating for sustained growth and development instead.

Stop graduating your new hires if you want them to also prioritize growth over mastery.

The Traditional View of Onboarding

Onboarding is often a structured and time-bound process aimed at acclimating new employees to their roles and your organization's culture.

This period typically spans from a few weeks to a few months, depending on the complexity of the role and the organization's operations. I've been on numerous teams that held a symbolic ceremony to mark the end of the new hire's onboarding. We celebrated the completion of their initial training and expected them to immediately start functioning independently. We treated them like they were experts before they had ever shown an ability to do the minimum expectations.

There are benefits to the traditional approach to onboarding, such as providing a clear structure and timeline. However, it also has significant adverse effects on the progression of the new hire's performance. When I help companies restructure their onboarding programs, these are the common challenges I see:

- **We give new hires a false sense of completion.** An "exit day" or a definitive drop-off day in new-employee training suggests that the employee no longer needs support, which is rarely the case. This is misleading to both the employee and their manager.
- **We neglect the need for ongoing development.** Ceasing onboarding often overlooks the necessity for ongoing training and development—which are both crucial for adapting to new challenges and technologies.
- **We create an environment that lacks long-term engagement.** Celebrating onboarding as a final achievement can lead to a decline in motivation and engagement once the initial excitement wears off.
- **We provide inadequate support systems.** Post-onboarding, employees may find themselves without the necessary support structures to continue their growth, leading to frustration and potential turnover.

Adopting a milestones-based approach to onboarding and employee development shifts the focus from a one-time event to a series of continuous achievements and developments. Milestones allow you to build performance by stacking the new hire's learning journey.

Types of Milestones

Milestones, simply put, are significant points of progress or achievements that mark various stages of employee development. Unlike a final onboarding graduation, milestones can occur at any time and at various levels of complexity and significance. They provide a framework for tracking progress, celebrating achievements, and ensuring continuous support and development. Milestones begin in onboarding, but they continue past this phase. Employees achieve milestones as they gain autonomy and deepen their knowledge within their role, opening them up to other opportunities to advance within the team or the organization. Milestones, however, are not agnostic to onboarding and other formal learning programs. Here are some milestone types:

- **New-hire milestones** include the successful completion of initial onboarding programs, such as understanding company operations and role-specific, day-to-day duties.
- **Skills acquisition milestones** focus on gaining the essential skills and knowledge required for the role, such as mastering specific technologies, processes, or durable skills.
- **Performance milestones** are based on achieving specific performance goals, such as completing a project, reaching sales targets, or receiving positive feedback from clients.
- **Professional development milestones** relate to ongoing learning and development, such as completing advanced training, obtaining certifications, or attending industry conferences.
- **Leadership milestones** include demonstrating leadership abilities, mentoring others, and contributing to significant process improvements.

Onboarding will encompass new-hire milestones until employees move into the next phases of everboarding. These milestones are unique to the role the employee was hired for, but this is their general makeup:

- Completion of initial training
- Initial goal setting and feedback session with leader

- Understanding the ecosystem (cross-functional teams and stakeholders)
- Proficiency in the role through performance assessments
- First formal review to assess goal and KPI progression
- Networking and cultural engagements

Celebrating Milestone Achievement

Celebrating milestones is crucial for maintaining motivation and engagement. It provides a sense of accomplishment and recognition, reinforcing the importance of continuous growth and development. Your organization's leaders need to understand how each member of their team likes to receive recognition before they start delivering it. Not everyone loves a large audience for public praise and it's important to know who feels this way. Recognition goes beyond verbal praise or an online platform.

Here are some ways to recognize your employee's achievements:

- **Public recognition.** Acknowledge achievements in team meetings, company newsletters, or on social media. Public recognition can boost morale and inspire others to strive for similar success.
- **Tangible rewards.** Offer rewards such as bonuses, gift cards, or extra vacation days. The reward should be meaningful and proportional to the significance of the milestone.
- **Professional development opportunities.** Provide opportunities for further professional development, such as additional training, attending conferences, or pursuing certifications. This not only rewards past achievements but also facilitates future growth.
- **Personalized celebrations.** Tailor celebrations to the individual's preferences and interests. This could include personalized thank-you notes, small gifts related to their hobbies, or a special lunch or dinner.
- **Team celebrations.** Celebrate milestones as a team to foster a sense of camaraderie and collective achievement. This can

involve team outings, celebratory meals, or fun activities that bring the team together.

As we covered at the beginning of this chapter, one adverse effect of onboarding graduations is the assumption that an employee has mastered all they need to know about how to do their job. Let's now focus on how to avoid that.

Avoiding the Pitfall of Early Mastery

Designing an onboarding process with the goal of early mastery can be detrimental to long-term employee development. Early mastery implies that employees are expected to quickly become experts in their roles, which can lead to unrealistic expectations, burnout, and disengagement. Instead, the focus should be on gradual and sustained development.

I frequently hear this discussion at industry conferences. We all seem to agree how detrimental this approach can be to our employees, but our actions don't always reflect our words. Many training programs still push rapid progression with steep consequences for lack of achievement. The reality is that we haven't adjusted many of the training program's expectations. Tracking new-hire progression helps us keep in touch with what's realistic and achievable and what's causing burnout and turnover.

High and unrealistic expectations for quick mastery can create undue pressure and stress. This leads to feelings of inadequacy and failure if employees cannot meet expectations. I've also seen the reverse happen. Early success is typically a result of luck and timing, which creates false expectations that the job will be easy because minimal effort led them to quick results.

As someone who has very closely tracked new-hire data for years, I can tell you with confidence how detrimental early success is to future success. Those who achieved results well ahead of the typical progression nearly always regressed shortly afterward and missed their next milestone achievement. In these situations, we must alert their manager to the importance of applying the role's fundamental skills to stay on track.

The pressure to achieve early mastery can also result in overwork and burnout, because employees may feel compelled to work long hours to keep up with demands. Burnout can have serious consequences, including decreased productivity and increased turnover.

I see this phenomenon most often in sales organizations. Whether you hire a seasoned pro or a fresh college grad, the journey to build their desk and hit their quota is long and gruesome and requires many hours. I once had a client with a hamster wheel hiring method, meaning they were hiring 100 new employees and losing 100 others in the same month. As we dug deeper into their processes, we found that one thing was glaringly out of alignment with their sales initiatives—their overtime policy.

Their sales employees are all hourly with a commission rate on top. Commission is how sales employees make their high rates of pay. The hourly rate is only considered a cushion to get them started and to supplement the down months that are inevitable in sales. As I mentioned, though, the journey to building a desk is a long one and demands many hours. Unfortunately, the expectation to hit their quota at all costs led to an underlying culture expectation to stay late every night. However, despite how late they stayed to hit their quota and not have their manager question their work ethic to get there, their overtime hours were never approved.

The organization attributed the high turnover levels to the talent acquisition's team ability to hire the right people with a "hungry" attitude needed for sales. With a gentle push, I was able to get them to coach their sales employees on more effective prospecting strategies, give them templates that get results, offer incentives for hitting their quota earlier in the week, and share how they should be spending their day. The point was to be more efficient with time in the office so they didn't have to stay late every day. Some late days are inevitable, but that can't be the expectation. Once these new processes were in place, turnover reduced by 51 percent in just 90 days.

Ultimately, when you focus on achieving early mastery, you are stifling employee growth. Everboarding is your vehicle to driving a growth culture in which mastery is never the goal. There will always be more to learn, more to apply, and more to change or remove. Focusing on early mastery leads to complacency, with less emphasis on continuous learning and development. Your employees will stop seeking new challenges, limiting their potential for growth, and your team will become a source of distractions that lack any value.

Designing for Sustained Development With Milestones

To avoid the pitfalls of early mastery, you can design your onboarding and development processes with sustained growth in mind.

Before offering best practices for implementing a milestones-based approach, take the short quiz in Figure 5-1 with your team to see where you excel and where you can make meaningful changes in designing for sustained development.

Figure 5-1.
Sustained Development Assessment Quiz

Instructions
For each statement, rate your agreement on a scale of 1 to 5, where 1 means "strongly disagree" and 5 means "strongly agree." After completing the quiz, tally your scores to see how well you're doing.

Questions	Score
1. Do we set realistic expectations?	
We clearly communicate to new hires that the onboarding process is just the beginning of their journey.	
We emphasize the importance of continuous learning and development.	
Employees understand that their growth is an ongoing process supported by the organization.	
2. Do we provide ongoing support?	
We ensure there are regular check-ins with employees to discuss their progress and challenges.	
Employees have access to necessary resources, such as training and development opportunities.	
Our team offers a supportive environment where help is readily available.	
3. Do we encourage practice and the ability to challenge the status quo?	
We foster a culture where practice is highly valued.	

Figure 5-1. *(continued)*

We provide opportunities for skill development, knowledge sharing, and innovation.	
Employees are encouraged to take on new challenges and explore different areas of interest.	
4. Do we promote a balanced work-life environment?	
We recognize the importance of offering consumable and accessible training for everyone.	
We remind managers to encourage their teams to take breaks, use their vacation time, and maintain a healthy lifestyle.	
Measures are in place to help prevent burnout and promote long-term well-being.	
5. Do we celebrate incremental progress?	
We recognize and celebrate small achievements.	
Celebrations and recognitions are timely and relevant to the milestones achieved.	
We reinforce the importance of continuous improvement by regularly acknowledging progress.	

Reflection

Based on your scores, identify specific areas where you can enhance your practices. Use the points provided in the quiz to guide your improvement. Sustained development is a continuous process, and ongoing efforts to support, develop, and recognize employees will lead to long-term success.

Initially, you may receive opposition to eliminating your formal graduation practices. Not all programs require this approach, but onboarding, without a doubt, does. A great implementation plan can put stakeholders' worries at ease. Incorporating a milestones-based approach requires careful planning, clear communication, and ongoing support.

Here are some steps you can take:
- **Define clear milestones** for each role and communicate them to employees.
- **Schedule regular check-ins** with employees to review progress, provide feedback, and adjust milestones as needed. They should be supportive and focused on development rather than evaluation. Their manager also needs to be present during these meetings.
- **Provide the resources** and support that employees need to achieve their milestones. This includes training programs, mentorship, tools, and technology.

Figure 5-1. *(continued)*

> - **Celebrate achievements** with meaningful recognition and rewards. Tailor celebrations to the individual's preferences and the milestone's significance.
> - **Regularly collect feedback** from employees in their first six months and then less frequently as time progresses. Use this feedback to make continuous improvements and ensure that the process remains relevant and effective.

To further expand on the benefits of using milestones rather than graduations, let's review two blended examples from clients I've worked with that demonstrate how companies can apply a milestone approach.

Company 1

Company 1 wanted to revamp its onboarding process to focus on milestones rather than a formal graduation and certification. Here are the steps it took:

- **Initial integration.** New hires participated in a two-week orientation program that included team-building activities, an introduction to Company 1's mission and values, and meetings with key stakeholders. The first milestone was completing this program and receiving a "Welcome to the Team" certificate.
- **Skills acquisition.** New developers were paired with mentors and given a list of essential technologies and tools to master. Each time a developer mastered a new technology, they received a badge and a small reward, such as a gift card.
- **Performance milestones.** Developers set quarterly performance goals in collaboration with their managers. Achieving these goals was celebrated with bonuses and public recognition during team meetings.
- **Professional development.** Company 1 encouraged continuous learning by providing a budget for professional development. Completing external certifications or attending industry conferences was celebrated with additional time off and financial support.
- **Leadership and innovation.** Employees demonstrating leadership potential were given the opportunity to lead projects or

mentor new hires. These contributions were recognized with special awards at the annual company event.

Company 2

Company 2 wanted to adopt a milestones-based approach to support the long-term development of its employees. Here are the steps it took:

- **Initial integration.** New hires completed a comprehensive onboarding program that included job shadowing, hands-on training, and an introduction to Company 2's culture and values. The initial milestone was completing this program and participating in a team welcome event.
- **Skills acquisition.** Employees were given personalized development plans outlining the skills and knowledge they needed to acquire. Each milestone was celebrated with certificates, recognition in the company newsletter, and small monetary rewards.
- **Performance milestones.** Employees set individual performance goals aligned with Company 2's strategic objectives. Achieving these goals was recognized with bonuses, public acknowledgment, and cross-training for potential advancement.
- **Professional development.** Company 2 supported ongoing learning by offering internal training programs, tuition reimbursement, and paid time-off for studying. Milestones in this area were celebrated with additional professional development opportunities and financial incentives.
- **Leadership and innovation.** Employees who took on mentoring, employee resource group facilitation, or contributed to innovative projects were recognized with leadership awards and special projects.

Both companies demonstrate how moving away from a rigid graduation or certification process can shift the focus toward continuous growth and incremental progress. This approach ensures that employees remain engaged and motivated over time, rather than becoming stagnant after an initial onboarding period. These case studies illustrate how a milestone-based framework fosters a sense of continuous achievement and belonging, keeping employees motivated at every stage of their journey.

The Role of Technology in Supporting a Milestones-Based Approach

Technology, particularly artificial intelligence (AI), plays a crucial role in supporting a milestones-based approach to onboarding and employee development. We live in a world where it is difficult to do our jobs without the right technology to support us. Not all the options I present here will be a fit for your team, and technology isn't always the answer; however, there are some powerful combinations you can leverage to push your initiatives forward effectively. Here are some forms of technology that your team can add to its tech stack to support a milestones-based approach:

- **Onboarding platforms** can streamline the process by providing a centralized hub for all onboarding activities. These platforms can track progress, provide access to training materials, and facilitate communication between new hires and their managers.
- **Learning management systems (LMSs)** can support continuous learning and development by offering a wide range of training programs, courses, and resources. They can also track employee progress and milestone completion.
- **Performance management tools** can help set and track performance goals, provide feedback, and recognize achievements. These tools can facilitate regular check-ins and ensure that employees are on track to achieve their milestones.
- **Collaboration tools** can enhance communication and teamwork, making it easier for employees to connect with colleagues, mentors, and managers. These tools can support the integration process and foster a sense of community.

- **Recognition platforms** can streamline the process of celebrating milestones by providing a platform for public recognition, rewards, and incentives. These platforms can also collect feedback and insights on the effectiveness of the recognition process.

Employee-Centric Future

The approach to onboarding and employee development is continually evolving, influenced by changes in technology, workforce demographics, and organizational needs. As our organizations recognize the diverse needs and preferences of employees, personalized onboarding experiences will become more common.

There will continue to be an increased focus on developing soft skills—such as communication, collaboration, and emotional intelligence—which are crucial for adapting to changing work environments and building effective teams. With the rise of remote and hybrid work models, organizations will need to adapt their onboarding processes to ensure that remote employees receive the same level of support and integration as their in-office counterparts.

The traditional approach to performance management is being replaced by continuous feedback and development. This milestones-based approach allows for more timely and relevant feedback, fostering a culture of ongoing improvement and growth. Onboarding is not the end of the journey—it's the beginning of an ongoing process of growth and development. By adopting a milestones-based approach, organizations can ensure that employees receive the support and recognition they need to thrive. Celebrating milestones, rather than viewing onboarding as a finite process, helps maintain motivation and engagement.

In this part of the book, we've covered several ways to shift your mindset and begin redefining employee development through the lens of your onboarding program. We started by providing new hires with the right support system and shifting to a people, not content, first approach. We then discussed tailoring your onboarding components to the needs of different segments of your new hires, part of which involves connecting them with performance-focused mentors and shifting from a one-size-all-fits approach. Last, we focused on implementing milestones, recognizing continuous development, and shifting from a graduation-based approach to onboarding. In the next part, we'll turn our attention to managers and your role in preparing them to receive the employee development baton from your training team.

Part 2
Manager-Led Development

CHAPTER 6
Securing Manager Involvement

Everboarding Myth #6
Managers don't have time for everboarding.

An everboarding strategy is impossible to execute unless you have well supported, prepared, and capable managers. Without adequate tools and resources, managers are operating and leading blindly. Because first impressions are vital for creating a strong, trusting relationship, managers can't appear disorganized or overwhelmed to their new employee.

How many hiring managers does your team support by onboarding their new employees?

That's the number of unique onboarding experiences taking place in your organization that you may (or may not) be measuring or tracking, and it's why collaboration and alignment with your managers is so critical. Onboarding is happening with or without you. Oftentimes, it's the latter because managers can't wait for perfection or total agreement from everyone involved to move forward and get their new employee performing independently.

No two managers are alike. Each comes with their own style, speed, and expectations for what good looks like. For that reason, you must approach every manager with empathy and intent to collaborate, not dominate. Give them a say and ultimately a voice in what onboarding, and beyond, looks like for their employees. If you don't include them, then you risk failure and here's why: Managers can control every facet of their team's life at work in varying degrees. They may control when their employees work, when they eat lunch, who they interact with, and how they're able to do their job. No matter how vast or narrow their influence may seem from the outside, start with the hiring managers before making any major decisions about how to revise your onboarding approach and implement your everboarding strategy. Their insights are gold.

Bear with me on this unconventional analogy. I like to think of managers as the goats of the organization. Yes, literal goats. Like goats navigating rocky terrain, managers operate in challenging environments, sandwiched between senior leadership and their teams. Just as goats are known for their agility and panoramic vision—thanks to those rectangular pupils—managers must balance the strategic directives from the top with the immediate needs of their employees. This unique position requires constant adaptability, awareness, and balance.

To effectively secure manager involvement in your everboarding strategy, begin by seeking first to understand your managers—their unique challenges, preferences, and expectations. Once you've gained this insight, focus on making change meaningful by aligning your strategy with their priorities and demonstrating tangible value for their teams. Then, leverage the change enablers you've been missing with the MOCCA Change Management Methodology (which we'll discuss later in this chapter) to equip managers to navigate transitions with clarity and confidence. These collectively create a foundation for collaboration and empower managers to lead with purpose and consistency.

Seek First to Understand Your Managers

Take time to understand who the managers are and what they care about. Ask them questions such as:

- **What makes you proud of your team?** Build a fortress around the manager's answer, and don't let anything change it. It can evolve, but that evolution should only happen within those walls. This is what keeps that manager motivated to show up each day for their team. Lean into it, but don't cause friction.

- **What does your team do really well?** Really dive into this one and get specifics. How do they do it really well? Is anyone on the team an exception? How long have they performed this task well? Be cautious of recency bias because you can't build standards off only a few months of success. Last, what would they like their team to do well, or is this it?
- **Who would you hate to lose the most?** Why? Understand the reason behind their answer. Many times, this employee is a top performer who can operate with total autonomy. Maybe it's simply someone the manager likes because they're steady with a positive attitude, which influences team culture. If it's the former, try to capture their persona. Is their process repeatable and scalable, or are they a purple squirrel?
- **Which obstacles does your team struggle with the most?** Why do you think that is? Their biggest obstacles are also barriers to their success. This is where you can be a hero. How can you help current and future employees? As a talent development leader, you have a unique advantage to be a bridge within your organization and likely know who can help or how the manager can fix this.
- **What does training on your team look like?** Do you save resources? Whether they have documented processes or they're training their employees in-the-moment, managers have something that needs to be uncovered by you. Their resources may also be helpful, so view this as an opportunity to curate useful materials and methods for other teams.

You're probably wondering if you should be the one capturing this information. Or, should it be one of your onboarding specialists? The answer is yes, to both. Of course, that may largely depend on the content governance strategy within your organization. Whoever makes the overarching strategic decisions must know these common practices and general sentiments.

Asking these questions and listening to and documenting the answers will help you establish trust and understanding as the one responsible for the strategic vision for everboarding. In fact, any other individual from your team who is hands on with developing employees also needs to establish a trusting relationship and needs to interact with your managers from time to time. As Henry Ford, industrialist and automotive engineer, is thought to have said, "Coming together is a beginning. Keeping together is progress. Working together is success."

Make Change Meaningful

Now that you have an awareness of what matters most to your managers and how they've been operating, it is time to jump in with a plan and make meaningful change for their teams. This is not the time to shy away from new ideas. Be bold and brave when crafting your vision for this partnership.

If you're building an onboarding—and eventually everboarding—program from the ground up, then congratulations on taking this big step forward! It's an exciting opportunity for you to take advantage of the lack of existing processes and content. You're in a great situation if you can create a system by designing and connecting processes, practices, and behaviors to one another and your entire organization. Be curious about all the processes already occurring in your organization by asking questions and gaining clarity. You can't build a system well, nor sustain it, on disjointed practices and processes.

Maybe you're not starting from scratch, and you already have a solid onboarding program in place. In this case, you likely want stronger involvement from your managers during the employee transition out of training-led onboarding. Are managers spending time correcting outdated onboarding practices? Are they totally hands off during formal onboarding?

Whatever is driving your need for change, it requires you to disrupt the status quo. Yes, it's a positive change, but change is still hard for everyone. With that said, be bold, and don't be afraid to ditch what no longer serves your organization.

Managing a complex change demands a well-thought-out plan, and that's what your managers deserve. There are so many change management models to choose from, but most are redundant. Ultimately, you need a handful of key components to implement an everboarding strategy. Your employees must feel these changes in short bursts instead of all at once. I find that the best organizations manage change with a systems approach that is built on adaptation, flexibility, and collaboration.

When systems fail, it's often because something was missing, broken, or used incorrectly. Think of a system like going to your local coffee shop to order a latte. You select your espresso style, choice of milk, syrup flavor, temperature, and cup size. The combinations are endless, but the final result depends on your personal selections, the barista preparing it, and the equipment functioning as designed. Imagine the shop only has blonde espresso available today, but you've been drinking dark espresso for a year. Your latte likely won't live up to your expectations. That one change took down the entire system you grew to love and rely on.

Over the years, I have observed that the changes that affect daily routines (like this latte example) are the hardest for employees to adjust to—not because of their size, but because of their frequency of use. They often have the lowest adoption rates when change is rolled out. Gaining and having autonomy in a role is valuable to any employee, and it is not something they will easily relinquish.

To keep your established systems from failing when one component changes, you need the right ingredients.

The Change Enablers You've Been Missing

During my years working in talent development, I have had the unique experience of always reporting to an executive. It has allowed me to be close to change initiatives and the monitoring process. I've seen what it takes to drive meaningful change across an organization as a direct report and later as a consultant.

Your everboarding strategy won't be an overnight success and it will not be easy to implement. This isn't meant to scare you, but to prepare you so you can get it right the first time. I missed the mark on my first attempt, and it all came down to leaving out the necessary change enablers. Figure 6-1 outlines those enablers in my MOCCA Change Management Methodology, which stands for motivation, optics, capabilities, communication, and assets.

Figure 6-1.
The MOCCA Change Management Methodology

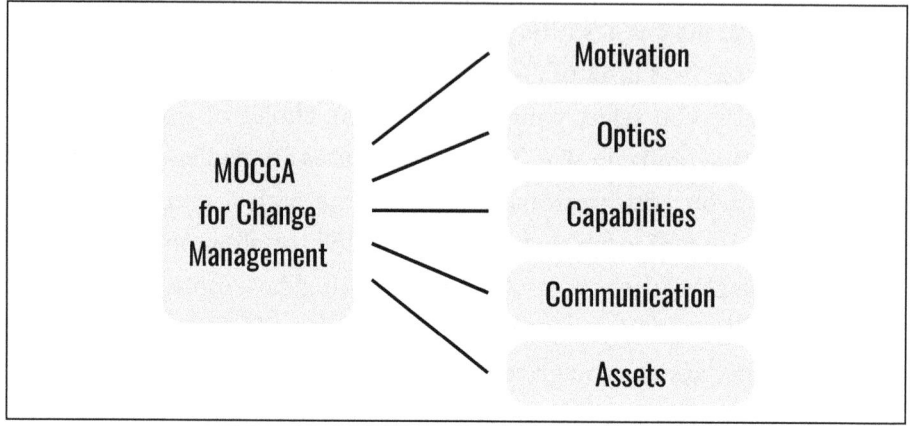

Motivation

The first crucial enabler of change is motivation. The motivation to change is not the employees' responsibility—it's their responsibility to be engaged. Any type of change is a distraction, and distracted employees are not engaged. Your managers are the key to motivating a change in behaviors or mindset, so include them in your plans. This doesn't mean you have to ask permission; you're simply bringing them along to offer perspective on how it can be done well.

I was at a midsize company years ago that was in the midst of massive growth. With that kind of growth comes lots of changes, and while most were exciting, others were in compensation plans, communication policies, and new roles that put more space between employees and senior leaders. We learned that the employees' voices mattered more than ever. Managers' voices, specifically, were lost in the shuffle, and we had to bring them back in to help us implement and manage change.

One thing that needs to be clear is that managers cannot motivate their employees to do their jobs well—despite that often being what they are expected to do. Instead, managers must model motivated behavior themselves to inspire motivation in their employees. Change is no exception. When I have included my organization's managers in change efforts, they've bought in to the new idea and in turn helped drive it. They adopted new changes to their day-to-day work, and their employees followed.

There's another thing to note about motivation: Resilience breathes life into it. Without resilience (the ability to overcome adversity) motivation doesn't exist. And without motivation, resilience serves no purpose. There is no world where the two are alone. When you develop a manager's ability to overcome adversity, you enable them to show up, motivated to drive change.

Take action: To motivate employees to engage in everboarding, managers need to be equipped with the right tools to inspire continuous growth. Start by involving managers early in the everboarding strategy planning process, giving them a clear understanding of their role in keeping employees engaged. Share the value of everboarding and fostering long-term career development. Here are two ways to ensure managers are properly motivated:

1. **Conduct a workshop with managers to discuss how to align developmental goals with their employees' personal aspirations.** Encourage managers to model motivation through their behavior—celebrating small wins and encouraging self-driven learning.
2. **Share data and success stories that demonstrate how everboarding leads to higher engagement, longer retention, and better employee performance.** This can help managers see the bigger picture of how motivation ties to their team's success.

Optics

The second enabler of change is optics. Ever heard the quote, "When there is no vision, there is no hope"? George Washington Carver said this, and it's incredibly fitting for your change efforts—especially when it comes to onboarding and everboarding strategies.

Employees must understand their role in the change. They need to know why their involvement is vital to the company's success and how their contributions fit into the bigger picture. This is particularly critical during onboarding, when employees are forming their initial impressions of the company's culture, priorities, and direction. Without a clear vision and alignment, onboarding risks becoming transactional and disjointed, eroding trust before you have a chance to build it.

Consider this: When launching an everboarding strategy, how you frame the initiative will dictate its success. Are you giving managers and employees a clear understanding of why they should prioritize continuous development? Are you painting a compelling picture of how this strategy contributes to individual growth and organizational success? If these optics aren't clear, your strategy may be misinterpreted, and rumors or misconceptions can easily derail progress.

For example, when I was at a large software company, there was a huge push for acquiring new technology capabilities to sell to our customers. Teams suddenly went from selling one or two products to selling an entire suite of solutions to new types of buyers. Compensation plans and quotas changed, and sellers were expected to quickly adapt. Yet no one explained the reason behind the change. Rumors circulated that the company was struggling financially or preparing to sell. In reality, the shift was driven by market trends and customer needs, but this vision was never shared. The result? A loss of trust in leadership, distracted employees, and significant turnover.

The lesson here is clear: Optics matter. Without a well-communicated vision, employees will fill in the gaps themselves—often with incorrect assumptions. In the context of onboarding and everboarding, this means ensuring that every new hire and tenured employee understands not just what they're learning, but why it matters. Connect the dots between their role, their growth, and the company's strategic goals to keep them engaged and aligned. Optics are not just about transparency—they're about inspiring trust and ensuring everyone is moving forward together.

Take action: To create alignment in your everboarding strategy, ensure all employees understand why continuous development matters. Clearly communicate the vision behind everboarding and why it isn't just an extended onboarding process, but a fundamental shift toward supporting employees' growth throughout their tenure. Here are two ways to ensure the optics of everboarding are clear:

1. **Host company-wide meetings to communicate your vision for everboarding.** Share how this strategy will directly affect employees' career growth, their opportunities for advancement, and the overall success of the company.
2. **Use visual aids like infographics or videos to explain the three phases of the everboarding model: onboarding, development, and refinement.** Make the optics clear to employees so they understand how their role and growth tie into the company's broader goals.

Communication

The third change enabler is communication. Employees need more than a Zoom recording or an email to navigate change, but not all changes should be delivered in the same sized package. A new onboarding program strongly supported by managers is an extra-large change. What that requires in terms of communication is far greater than the messaging for having sellers follow a new ordering process, for example.

I recommend using agreed upon "cup sizes" to determine the impact of a change and the type of communication necessary to support it. Thinking about changes in terms of cup sizes can help you document what communication and engagement methods you'll need to use for the different kinds of changes your team implements.

Here are some examples:

- **Small changes** could include making a new field available in customer profiles, introducing a new submission form for internal employee referrals (instead of emailing them to HR), and requiring passwords to be changed every 90 days.

- **Medium changes** include introducing a new resource to send to prospects, enabling multifactor authentication, and adding a new question to a one-on-one form for managers.
- **Large changes** include requiring critical process changes in how vendors are invoiced, introducing a new escalation process for customer sentiments, and adding a new role to the project management team.
- **Extra-large changes** include rolling out a new recognition tool, navigating company-wide layoffs, and switching software programs from Teams to Zoom.

My former executive team engaged in this discussion before any new change rollout to decide how large the change was. We would ask one another, "What size of cup does this change need?" Table 6-1 offers an example of our change chart.

Table 6-1.
Example Change Chart

Cup Size	Email	Resource Creation	Standalone Meeting	Training Program
S	X			
M	X	X		
L	X	X	X	
XL	X	X	X	X

We used these general guidelines when making change management decisions. However, each change gets a unique chart as needed. Some changes may also require one-on-one conversations, manager training, or another niche situation that the general guidelines don't address.

Take action: Communication is the key to your everboarding strategy being understood and embraced across the organization. Implement clear communication channels for employees at all stages of their journey and establish feedback loops so employees know where they stand and how they can continue to grow. Here are two ways to ensure your communication is effective:

1. **Create a communication plan that details how you will share everboarding updates and check-ins with employees** (such as monthly progress reports, team meetings, or manager check-ins). Regular communication will help maintain momentum and build trust in the strategy.
2. **Encourage two-way communication for managers and employees to regularly engage in development conversations.** Provide resources, such as templates for managers to use during feedback sessions, that focus on continuous development rather than just performance reviews.

Capabilities

The fourth enabler of change is capabilities. To successfully implement an everboarding strategy, employees need specific skills and knowledge that will allow them to not only understand the core aspects of the onboarding process but also engage in continuous development over time. These capabilities include:

- **Understanding the everboarding framework.** Employees, especially managers, must have a clear grasp of what everboarding is, how it differs from traditional onboarding, and why it's important for long-term growth. This involves understanding the three phases of the everboarding strategy (onboarding, development, and refinement).
- **Continuous learning mindset.** Employees need to adopt a mindset that values ongoing learning and development, viewing their role in a company as an evolving journey. Managers must support this mindset by integrating learning opportunities into daily work and modeling continuous development behavior.
- **Feedback and self-assessment skills.** For everboarding to work, employees need to be able to assess their own progress and seek regular feedback. Managers need to provide constructive feedback

in a manner that promotes growth, not just at the beginning of an employee's journey, but throughout their time with the company.
- **Manager competency in leading development.** Managers must be able to foster development and engagement beyond the onboarding phase. They need to be skilled at identifying individual development needs, integrating continuous learning into day-to-day operations, and fostering an environment that supports long-term employee growth. Without manager buy-in and competency, the everboarding strategy will fail.
- **Technological proficiency.** For a seamless experience, employees need to be comfortable using the LMS, tracking tools, and other resources that support continuous development. They must know where to find learning resources, how to track progress, and how to leverage technology to enhance their development.

If these capabilities are not identified, tracked, and developed, employees will resist the change, underperform, or be unaware of how to progress within the everboarding framework. This is why it's important to assess employees' skills early on, particularly managers' capabilities, so you can tailor your training and resources accordingly.

To ensure successful implementation, track the application of these capabilities over time. This requires using preassessments, surveys, or face-to-face conversations to gauge where employees stand and to identify gaps. By slowing down and meeting employees where they are, you'll avoid reactive training later on, making the transition smoother and more effective in the long run.

Take action: For everboarding to succeed, employees and managers need the skills and knowledge to sustain the process. This includes specific technical and soft skills to support continuous development. Here are two ways to ensure you have the right capabilities in place:

1. **Identify the key skills and competencies employees need to continually grow in their roles and create personalized development plans.** For new employees, ensure that their

development plan is aligned with their onboarding process and tracks how they transition into the everboarding journey.
2. **Equip managers with training to effectively support ongoing employee development.** This may include leadership training, coaching skills, and tools to identify employees' developmental needs.

Assets

The fifth, and final, enabler of change is assets like resources, collateral, and technology. Employees at all levels should have what they need to successfully adopt and implement a change, but this will vary greatly by team and individual.

Depending on the size of the change, managers may need a support toolkit that includes resources such as a new one-on-one template, technology infographics, or explainer videos. Surround your new change with valuable assets that managers can lean on for refreshers and reinforcements.

Assets can be separated into three types:
1. **Skim assets** are essential for onboarding and initial everboarding phases, when quick, accessible information is necessary to get employees aligned and up to speed.
2. **Swim assets** are perfect for employees in the development phase of everboarding, when they need more context, resources, and deeper understanding of how their roles are evolving.
3. **Dive assets** are best suited for the refinement phase of everboarding, when employees are expected to take full ownership of their roles and career development. These assets will provide detailed instructions and comprehensive guidance to ensure employees are equipped to navigate complex scenarios related to continuous development and leadership responsibilities.

Take action: Provide the right resources and tools to support everboarding at every stage of the employee journey. These assets help both employees and managers easily track progress, access learning materials, and reinforce key behaviors. Here are two ways to ensure you have the right assets:

1. **Develop a centralized resource hub that houses training materials, development tools, and progress trackers for both employees and managers.** Make it easy for employees to access relevant training resources that will support their ongoing development, and ensure managers have tools to track progress and provide feedback.
2. **Curate assets based on the role and phase of development.** For example, new hires might need foundational knowledge assets (skim), while tenured employees may need deeper, role-specific materials (swim or dive). Offer a variety of learning resources to meet employees where they are in their development journey.

Managing the complex change of an everboarding strategy isn't only about the employees; it's also about the stakeholders you must align with. Managing and implementing change can't be done with any gaps. Each program within your everboarding strategy must be managed like the MOCCA Change Management Methodology outlined in this chapter. If you prioritize your optics, define capabilities, effective communication, and supportive assets, then you will set yourself up for success to see the change transform your employee development experience.

Keep Managers Engaged in Everboarding

This chapter emphasized the importance of collaboration, empathy, and providing managers with the right tools and resources to succeed. Securing their involvement is necessary for the success of your everboarding strategy. Managers are a catalyst in shaping the employee experience, and without their active participation and support, the strategy is bound to fail. By taking time to understand each manager's unique challenges, strengths, and expectations, you can tailor the everboarding approach to better align with their needs.

CHAPTER 7
Preparing Your Managers

Everboarding Myth #7
It's just on-demand learning.

One of the most common myths about everboarding is that it's simply an on-demand learning model. This oversimplification fails to account for the intricate systems and human interactions required to sustain a culture of growth. While on-demand learning can be a tool, it is far from the full picture.

This phase of your everboarding strategy requires a systems thinking approach. Daniel Kim (1999), co-founder of the MIT Center for Organizational Learning, defines a system as "any group of interacting, interrelated, or interdependent parts that form a complex and unified whole that has a specific purpose. Without such interdependencies we have just a collection of parts, not a system."

Once onboarding is over, employees enter a phase of "on-demand" learning. For many talent development teams, this is a way to address the need to continue workplace learning and skill acquisition while compromising with the manager's desire to not have work interrupted by formal training.

Traditionally, talent development teams have created a library of on-demand content for employees to access whenever they want. They may even provide managers with assessments for their employees, track progress and competency in an LMS or performance management tool, and then measure its effectiveness over time.

If only it were that easy. Nothing about developing adults in the workplace is easy. Humans are complex and so are their motivators. More than likely, employees won't make time for learning unless it leads to a promotion, money, or praise—or worse, because they're on a PIP and desperate to turn it around.

Employees aren't the only ones you need to be concerned with. Their managers will likely demonstrate unconscious bias, assess their employees differently, and unfortunately think your training and development efforts have become yet another box to check on their long list of tasks. Your team can easily become a source of stress rather than a resource for success.

How do you overcome this? This chapter covers how to enable your managers (not just train them) to implement an everboarding strategy by equipping them with the relevant skills to be better people leaders. They influence every single part of the employee experience, controlling schedules, priorities, goals, and resources. For that reason, they must become coaches and forego the process-centric approach they've grown comfortable with: one-on-ones completed, orders approved, forecast turned in, tasks reassigned, repeat. Your focus should be on helping them identify their team's behaviors and needs to promote development instead of maintenance activities.

Great Managers Are Great Teachers

If you want managers to become better people developers, you must develop their ability to teach and motivate. They need to understand, demonstrate, and teach the critical skills their employees need to succeed.

Supporting managers to be better teachers is a lot like the approach I have taken with personal training clients. They are so similar that I call it the personal trainer method (Figure 7-1). This framework gives managers the support they need and includes all the elements of a people development strategy. The personal trainer method empowers managers to not only manage but also mentor and develop their teams effectively, driving continuous improvement and fostering a culture of growth within the organization.

Figure 7-1.
The Personal Trainer Method for Supporting Managers

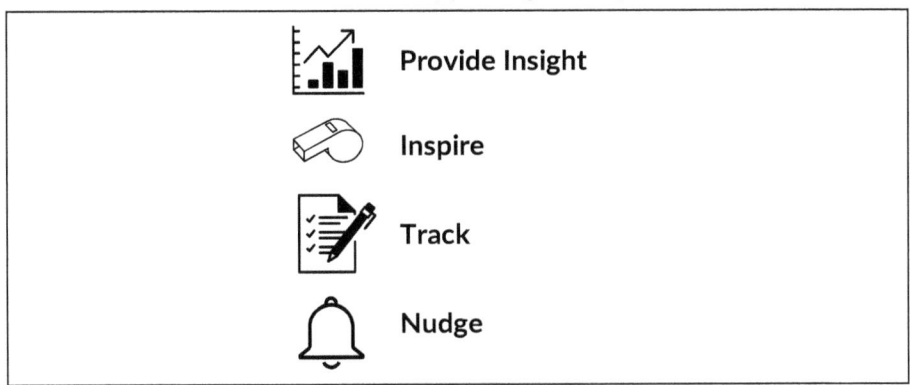

The personal trainer method includes the following actions:
- **Provide insight.** Give managers the essential data and information they need to make informed decisions and effectively guide their teams. This includes access to relevant metrics, performance analytics, and insights into individual and team dynamics.
- **Inspire.** Using a universal coaching model, equip managers with a structured approach to skill development and coaching. This model serves as a foundation for fostering growth and maximizing the potential of each team member through personalized guidance and support.
- **Track.** Provide a designated platform for managers to document and track their coaching conversations and progress. Whether it's a shared folder for simplicity or sophisticated performance management software for comprehensive tracking, this ensures accountability and continuity in the coaching process.
- **Nudge.** To support ongoing engagement and consistency, integrate gentle reminders and prompts into the framework. These nudges serve as friendly reminders for managers to follow up on action plans, celebrate milestones, or address challenges proactively.

Great Managers Overcome Adversity

The hardest lesson most new managers have to learn is that they cannot motivate their team. Motivation comes from within, and try as you might, you cannot motivate other people. However, managers can model motivated behavior, which is the real expectation you must have. This involves using empathy and encouragement and understanding what drives others to help them stay motivated and perform at their best.

Develop your managers' ability to take their team to greater heights by supporting their emotional intelligence and motivational awareness and teaching them how to leverage their employees' motivational awareness. Start with:

- **Self-awareness.** Managers should be able to recognize and understand their own motivations, desires, strengths, and weaknesses. This can help them understand what drives their employees, what goals they value, and how their emotions and motivations influence their behavior.
- **Emotional regulation.** Managers should be able to manage and control their frustration, disappointment, or excitement and be able to stay focused on goals and maintain motivation despite setbacks. They should model emotional regulation so employees can understand what this looks like in action and repeat it.
- **Adaptability.** Managers should be flexible and adaptable in adjusting goals and motivations based on changing circumstances or feedback. Great managers can pivot their focus and efforts as needed without losing motivation or momentum.

What most manager programs are missing is practice to develop these skills. The more you can put them into challenging scenarios to overcome, the better their response will be. It requires practice to take a terrible situation and turn it into a positive one or an opportunity. Build their resilience and help them build their confidence; it'll spread like wildfire.

The entire purpose of everboarding is to sustain a culture of growth for all employees to prosper. Motivation is a key part of cultivating a growth mindset, which is crucial for developing the characteristics of a great leader. After all, behavior is not just about doing something, but doing it with purpose and without fear, overcoming adversity, embracing change, and acting with confidence.

Manager Toolkit

Creating a toolkit specifically for guiding managers in developing new hires alongside the training team involves incorporating various elements to ensure the tools are practical, engaging, and effective. The toolkit should be accessible in the moment of need. You must collaborate with HR to include vital information for hiring and developing employees. The toolkit should provide a centralized location for managers to access what they need to complete those talent-related tasks, including those for hiring, interviewing, training, and onboarding.

Manager guidance for hiring and interviewing may include:
- Compensation policies
- Requesting an open job requisition
- Writing a job description
- Interviewing best practices
- Interview process information
- Applicant tracking system (ATS) instructions
- Onboarding schedule
- Hiring dates
- Tool access request forms
- Making an offer

Manager guidance for training and onboarding may include:
- Day one instructions
- Forms
- Microsoft Office troubleshooting
- Teams FAQs
- Salesforce FAQs
- HR or benefits department information

Transforming Managers Into Growth Leaders

This chapter dismantled the myth that everboarding is merely on-demand learning and redefined it as a comprehensive system for sustained employee development. It emphasized the critical role managers play in this strategy, highlighting their influence over every aspect of the employee experience. By equipping managers with the skills necessary to become effective coaches through frameworks like the personal trainer method, you can foster a culture of continuous growth.

CHAPTER 8
Evaluating New-Hire Success

Everboarding Myth #8
Everboarding is just a replacement for performance management.

One of the most significant advantages of everboarding is the amplification of the talent development team's voice within the organization. As your team shifts from a reactive to a proactive role, you gain greater visibility and influence over business strategies. This allows your team of professionals to engage with key stakeholders, aligning training initiatives with broader organizational goals and demonstrating their influence on business outcomes. This alignment not only enhances the perceived value of the talent development function in your organization but also positions it as an indispensable partner in driving business success.

In the spirit of alignment, your frontline managers will continue to be your biggest mobilizers internally. Helping them measure and understand data for their new employees' success means taking a strong, strategic approach to your partnership. Neither of you can support the new employee alone, or your tenured population. Know going into this partnership that managers will have different views. They may have a different idea of determining new employee success. Let the data speak for itself and don't rely on opinions and gut instincts to build trust with them.

Begin with the end in mind. If you don't know where you're going, you can't map out how to get there. New employees need a road map to success that is based on achievable metrics and realistic expectations. Clear communication around these should start right away to avoid disappointment and confusion.

Each role at your organization must have clear key performance indicators (KPIs). No one wants to be in a role in which their value is not known, and KPIs can offer that clarity. Help managers recognize that KPI discussions must happen before employees ever begin working at your organization, and they are a part of any good interview process.

In this chapter, we explore the critical components that contribute to manager alignment and the talent development team's role in driving success, equipping managers to assess and support their new hires, facilitating effective one-on-ones, and creating a sustainable playbook for long-term success. Together, these elements form a cohesive approach to measuring and improving the outcomes of your new-hire initiatives, building a stronger partnership between the talent development team and managers.

Your Role in New-Hire Success

Is onboarding a direct line to new-hire performance? Not necessarily. In addition, while KPIs are important, they're often achieved well after traditional onboarding ends. Onboarding is a stepping stone, or a foundation, for an employee's future performance, but it takes a village to get them there. Instead, consider acquiring and documenting your own new-hire data, which is crucial for your team's ability to identify, track, and share insights with upper management and frontline managers. An employee's first year on the job is spent assimilating, gaining autonomy, and striving toward their KPIs. In addition to the KPIs monitored by their manager, your team will also be collecting vital new-hire data, and it might tell a much different story.

New-hire data points show the new employee's efforts, attitude, and potential, which helps your team show the value of onboarding it provides and demonstrate where new hires can see progress before their outcomes are achieved. It keeps both parties engaged in their work.

For example, if a handful of business development representatives are going through your onboarding program, their manager would be tracking the number of demos they book and their stage conversion. While your team would care about those metrics, you'd care more about their behaviors, which could include the number of outbound dials made, how many connections resulted in a booked demo, time between calls, documentation, and application of feedback.

The biggest difference between what you care about and what their manager cares about is the application of what they've learned to get desired performance results. Their manager is focused on the performance results (or the KPIs). Best practices and the consistent application of them will lead to desired results. Measuring those behaviors is necessary for understanding the effectiveness of your onboarding efforts.

Part of that measurement is also asking for feedback from the employees on how their job is going, what needs to be improved, and what needs to be removed for them to get results. From here, you can work with their manager to identify what reinforcement looks like. This open communication keeps agility top of mind and employees are able to quickly pivot with you. It helps them understand that change can only happen if you move forward together, so including their voice in change is the ultimate catalyst.

I have spent a lot of time with sales teams that demand to measure every behavior and its impact on performance. At a midsize software company, I was working with the VP of sales to highlight how new-hire evaluation data can bridge the gap between onboarding efforts and long-term performance. One manager had a habit of assessing his team primarily based on recent results—how many demos were booked that week or their conversion rates. When new sales development representatives (SDRs) struggled to hit those metrics early on, he often labeled them poor fits for the role.

However, my team had been tracking a different set of data. For one SDR, Hannah, the numbers told a more nuanced story. While her demo bookings were low, her behavioral metrics—such as outbound call volume, the percentage of calls resulting in meaningful conversations, and her ability to incorporate feedback into her pitch—showed consistent progress. She was putting in the work and improving steadily.

When my team shared this data with her manager, it challenged his perception. It took several points of data beyond one new hire, but he began to see that they weren't failing; this was part of the learning curve. He started having more developmental one-on-ones with his newest employees and providing targeted feedback on behaviors instead of solely pushing for results.

This is why it's essential to collect and analyze new-hire data beyond standard KPIs. Without this approach, recency bias could lead to prematurely losing a high-potential employee. By showing managers how to assess behaviors and not just their performance outcomes, you can become a partner in both new-hire success and manager growth.

When I provide an assessment for managers to complete, I also provide guidance to ensure that every employee is assessed adequately. We often use the same assessments for an employee with 90 days of tenure as an employee with one year. Expectations for performance need to be realistic based on experience levels at the company.

Table 8-1 provides an example of assessment guidance.

Table 8-1.
Manager Guidance and Support for Assessing Employees

Employee Tenure	Assessment Focus Areas	Manager Guidance and Support
0–3 months	• Assimilation into the company culture • Mastery of foundational knowledge • Early behavioral indicators (e.g., learning pace, engagement, and curiosity)	• Schedule weekly one-on-ones to address questions and provide encouragement. • Set clear short-term goals focused on learning milestones. • Provide frequent feedback and recognize small wins to build confidence. • Pair with a buddy or mentor for additional support.

Table 8-1. *(continued)*

4–6 months	• Application of learned skills • Building independence in tasks • Early KPI indicators (e.g., output volume and time management)	• Transition to biweekly one-on-ones focusing on skill refinement and goal alignment. • Use behavioral metrics to identify strengths and gaps. • Encourage peer-to-peer collaboration to build team integration. • Discuss alignment between individual progress and role expectations.
7–12 months	• Consistency in performance • Progress toward full ownership of responsibilities • Early-stage contributions to team goals	• Shift focus to refining skills and improving efficiency. • Conduct monthly development-focused one-on-ones, incorporating stretch goals. • Provide feedback on contributions to team projects and discuss opportunities for greater impact. • Begin exploring long-term career goals and aspirations.
1 year	• Full accountability for role KPIs • Leadership potential or advanced skill development • Engagement and retention indicators	• Use quarterly one-on-ones to focus on long-term growth and career development. • Encourage participation in cross-functional projects or leadership development programs. • Identify challenges or barriers to sustained engagement. • Provide opportunities for upskilling and professional advancement.

Supporting Managers With Assessing Their New Hires

Measuring and evaluating the effectiveness of new-hire development requires collaboration with frontline managers, but their plates are full. Take the lead here instead of adding another item to their plate; help them see the benefit in measuring beyond their new employee's KPIs. Managers all have different experience levels with hiring and developing new employees. Each will require you to adjust your approach according to their experience.

Create a shared space where employee data is available to your team and the manager responsible for the new hire. In the past, I have let managers have visibility into new-hire data for everyone we hired on the same date as their employee. It helped them see how their new hire compared with their peers rather than comparing their employee to someone more tenured. Due to employer confidentiality expectations, this may not be an approach you can take. In that case, you can offer broad, not individual, data for managers to analyze. Share how new hires have performed overall in their respective division and help managers understand if their employee is performing at the average rate of productivity for new hires.

Key Performance Indicators

KPIs will be the most important data points to the manager, so go ahead and add them to your new-hire dataset too. After all, KPIs capture what the new employees were hired to do, and you'll need to know whether they're on track to achieve them. Eventually, this will become the most important data and strongest indicator of success, but remember these are outcomes, not behaviors. Early days in a new job are spent fumbling through tasks, and you must first ensure new hires learn good habits remove any poor ones. Outcomes are desired but can't be required until the right habits are formed from formal training.

Objectives and Key Results

Objectives and key results (OKRs) are a powerful framework for collaboratively setting goals and tracking performance with employees and their managers. (I explained more about them in chapter 3.) OKRs strike a good balance between what's ambitious and what's achievable, but they require regular check-ins to ensure completion. They are very effective for an environment with well-aligned managers and talent development staff so new hires can get guidance from their success team (which we discussed in chapter 2).

Work with managers to craft OKRs that are specific to each individual new hire. These are not meant to be universal. An everboarding strategy is best implemented with clear up-front expectations, as we've discussed all along. Tailoring OKRs gives new hires the best chance at success in your organization. Not every manager will feel comfortable establishing OKRs or taking the lead on them. I have found that a short training course on creating OKRs helps tentative managers immensely. I can't stress the importance of preparing managers for the tasks you're asking them to perform.

Engagement Level

Another measurement you must consider for new hires is engagement level. At the end of each week—after their coach, manager, or mentor has met with the new hire—ask each one to rate the new hire's perceived level of engagement. Define what that means to your team.

This partnership can create a seamless and effective everboarding experience—from onboarding to beyond—that sets new hires up for success and accelerates their integration into the organization.

Quality of Work

Quality of work is an essential measurement that you'll need to evaluate new hires on. Not only is the talent development team teaching best practices, but managers are reinforcing them and the new hire's performance-focused mentors (from part 1) are also supporting quality work. I've spent a lot of time with sales teams, and a common qualm from their support teams and senior leaders is the lack of proper work output documentation. After all, the data you have is only as good as the people inputting it, and not every company has tools to automate documentation. Most have to rely on their employees to provide accurate data, and it's frustrating to lack confidence in your close rates, product performance, and seller effectiveness (or whatever measures of performance you use).

New hires are consuming massive amounts of information in their early days, and without reinforcement, they will form undesirable habits. Take time to audit their work and review it with them weekly. Give them frequent feedback in the beginning so they don't need corrections later. Senior leaders appreciate good data hygiene (or accurate, reliable data).

When I ran an onboarding program for a medical staffing company, my team split new hires up and assigned each a coach to review their weekly progress. Their manager and mentor were invited to attend these meetings as well, so the employee had a whole team of people working to support them. We reviewed documentation each week, along with their attitude, efforts, and production. Documentation was a crucial part of our business because we needed to note every conversation and store credentials in case we were ever questioned by an outside authority on our hiring decision for a candidate.

It's hard for most managers to be receptive to documenting new-hire data because they're focused on getting these employees to full productivity as quickly as possible. They don't necessarily want to slow down and consider the drivers of productivity. There is also a lot of pressure on your team to rapidly get these employees productive and then reduce your involvement. Set realistic expectations with your managers and other stakeholders about their commitment to documentation.

Using a combination of objective and quantifiable criteria is essential for effectively evaluating quality of work, especially when assessing new hires. Objective criteria refer to specific, observable standards or benchmarks that can be measured without bias. Quantifiable metrics are specific measurements that provide clear insights into performance and progress. This approach helps provide a fair evaluation that is based on measurable outcomes and performance metrics.

Here's an example of some criteria you could you use in a new hire evaluation:

- **Evaluate new hire's perceived engagement on a scale of 1 to 5.**
    - Rate the new hire's engagement level based on their interactions, enthusiasm, and responsiveness.

- **Assess behavioral metrics.**
  - Is the new hire demonstrating curiosity and a willingness to learn?
  - Are they applying feedback effectively to their work?
  - Are they proactive in seeking help or clarifications when needed?
- **Measure job-specific skills and competencies.**
  - Is the new hire meeting early milestones tied to their role?
  - Have they shown improvement in their foundational skills since starting?
  - Are they demonstrating the ability to work independently?
- **Review quantifiable performance metrics.**
  - Is the new hire meeting initial KPIs or benchmarks specific to their role?
- **Address gaps and next steps.**
  - Have gaps in skills, engagement, or performance been identified?
  - Are there actionable next steps for improvement, including additional training or mentorship?

Supporting Managers With One-on-Ones

If you want a direct route to improving performance, start with the managers' one-on-ones. Just because your organization has a framework in place for those conversations doesn't mean managers like it and are using it. More often than not, they're simply checking boxes. I believe in giving managers the flexibility to coach with their heart and good intentions, while providing guard rails to keep them focused on development and connection with their employee. Don't leave it to chance and don't expect them to adopt a new framework without reservations.

As a former sales manager and talent development manager, I've experienced how different it is to manage these two audiences. What worked for my sales team didn't always work for my talent development team. I needed better one-on-one best practices that could narrow down what to discuss, a flow to follow, and what to avoid. Most importantly, anything I created needed to have only two action items so employees wouldn't leave each meeting feeling overwhelmed.

The FOCUS Framework—which stands for feedback, objectives, challenges, understand, and support—was born from these core beliefs. It equips frontline managers with a simple yet effective tool to drive engagement, development, and results, while making their interactions more meaningful and aligned with both individual and company goals.

This framework provides a clear structure for one-on-ones, ensuring managers cover essential areas such as feedback, OKRs, challenges, and the need for support. I have seen this consistency help frontline managers conduct effective and purposeful meetings without feeling overwhelmed by where to start.

F: Feedback

Feedback is a skill that many managers struggle with, but just like anything else, the more you practice, the better you get. It's not a nice-to-have skill; it's a crucial one that will always be a part of a manager's day-to-day experiences. By regularly focusing on how to deliver feedback, frontline managers can address performance issues early and recognize achievements promptly. This leads to quicker course corrections and more motivated, engaged team members.

Here are some tips for managers:
- Provide ongoing, constructive feedback on recent performance and growth areas.
- Keep feedback about positive reinforcement and areas for improvement balanced.
- Use the BEST Feedback Model (that we covered in chapter 4) when providing feedback.

O: Objectives

With objectives as a key part of the discussion, managers can ensure their team members' goals align with organizational priorities. This fosters accountability and ensures that even day-to-day tasks contribute to larger company goals. Accountability will make or break a team's culture and performance levels; without it, they are working aimlessly.

Here are some tips for managers:
- Discuss short- and long-term performance and learning goals or established OKRs.
- Align these objectives with the team's goals and the company's mission or current objectives.

C: Challenges

Addressing challenges directly helps create a proactive culture in which problems are dealt with openly and quickly. Frontline managers can anticipate and mitigate small issues before they escalate, maintaining team morale and productivity.

Here are some tips for managers:
- Identify any current challenges or roadblocks.
- Collaboratively brainstorm solutions or resources to overcome these obstacles.

U: Understand

Understanding requires managers to regularly check in on their team members' well-being and engagement. This strengthens relationships, builds trust, and increases retention, which is crucial in frontline positions that can have high turnover. If your frontline managers haven't had emotional intelligence (EQ) or diversity, equity, and inclusion (DEI) training, they may find this element challenging at first. Incorporate training and support groups for those skills for maximum impact.

Here are some tips for managers:
- Seek to understand your team members' perspectives.
- Ask open-ended questions to understand their work experience, career aspirations, or personal challenges.

S: Support

Focusing on support helps managers be more intentional in providing the right resources, coaching, or guidance. It also keeps them accountable for following up, creating a more growth-oriented environment. When managers feel the demand to provide support, they are more likely to do it.

Here are some tips for managers:
- Offer support as needed, whether that's mentorship, resources, or professional development opportunities.
- Commit to actionable steps that you'll take as a leader to help your team members succeed, and have them commit to two realistic actions that you will review in your next one-on-one.

Establish a Playbook for Sustainability

I often hear from folks that securing such involved manager support would never work in their company or industry. I have to strongly disagree. Like every other idea or framework within this book, you may need to adjust it to meet your organization where it is. A playbook is something you must work toward to keep alignment after you've gained it.

I have walked into a "Disneyland of training" where I had complete support and buy-in to provide learning to employees, mostly through in-person training, while the company was rapidly growing. I have also walked into an organization where no one wanted to see me, ever, unless I was giving away cash for pub trivia. And I have seen everything in between. I promise, you aren't the first to think, "This will never work here." However, there is always a way. You may have to start small, or plant the seed over and over again, but it is always worth the effort.

Start with one team, if you must, to prove the effectiveness and value that strong manager support can bring to continued new-hire success. That's what many of my clients and peers have had to do, but the benefits are worth it!

The manager toolkit described in chapter 7 provides guidance on the tasks they need to complete to get a new employee through the door, set that employee up to do their job, and ensure they complete HR-required compliance items. The manager playbook, on the other hand, is not about tasks; it's a guide for development and coaching and the challenges that come with them. The playbook keeps managers involved in new-hire development in a consistent way. It ensures that every new hire is given the same chance at success because their experiences won't change like the wind. Your playbook should create alignment between you and the manager on who completes what and when.

Figures 8-1 and 8-2 offer examples of what you may include in your manager playbook, using weeks 1 and 4 to demonstrate the expectations managers should have for their employees and themselves.

Figure 8-1.
Example Manager Playbook for Week 1

Class Objectives
- Welcome!
- Computer setup, access to systems, and daily processes (such as logging in)
- New hire compensation plan review
- New hire sales tracker (including introduction and how to use)
- Corporate training on understanding the company history, using "biz" and "con" databases, and running counts on Genie and .com Sales process training on buyer personas (such as understanding what clients look like, their common pain points, and how to solve their problems) and crucial questions (including understanding their importance and how to use them)
- Resource training on Outlook (including creating an email and accepting a calendar invite), Teams (including creating chats and updating status), Spekit (including using the search and favorite functions), and Mindtickle (including accessing and completing assigned modules)

Manager Checklist (Role-Specific Training)
- Introduce new hire to team.
- Review role expectations.
- Review division policies and expectations.
- Add new hire to Teams channel.
- Add new hire to the team distribution list.
- Add new hire to team meetings.
- Define working hours.

Figure 8-2.
Example Manager Playbook for Week 4

Class Objectives
- Specialty database training on when to sell and where the data is (such as new mover, new business, doctors and dentists, churches, occupation, auto data, B2C link, and bankruptcy)
- IDMS and broker requests (including when to use and how to request)
- Competitor review

Manager Checklist
- Weekly one-on-one. Discuss what reinforcement or retraining topics are needed.
- Review specialty databases. Ask rep for examples of when they could sell each and where the data is located (for example, .com, Genie, or IDMS).
- Spot check Salesforce notes and follow-ups. Give rep feedback on what they are doing well and coach them on what they can improve.
- Forecast with new hire.
- Account transitions. Build view in Salesforce and review processes. When are they assigned? When do they need to be completed by? What is the process to mark them as transitioned? What is their goal when reaching out to each transition?
- Manager side-by-side demo of calling regs
- Manager "side saddle" to watch new hire work leads
- Listen to calls and provide coaching using the call coaching form

---

Data Axle created this playbook to give managers guidance on onboarding their new employees, and to serve as a mechanism for alignment because the objectives, action items, and tools were agreed upon by both the talent development team and the hiring managers. This is an evolving source of truth for your team to ensure that every new hire is set up for success with consistency in training delivery and clarity for the managers.

Creating a playbook for managers on how to interact with, develop, and coach new employees until they are fully autonomous is a strategic project that can bring significant benefits to your talent development team. Following this approach not only ensures the smooth integration of new hires but also provides a road map for sustainable growth and long-term employee success.

Ensures Consistency

First, the manager playbook introduces consistency into the organization's employee development process. When all managers are aligned on how to onboard and coach new hires, the organization can deliver a uniform experience across departments and teams. Every employee, regardless of their manager, receives the same level of support and guidance. You create equality so everyone gets the same chance to succeed.

By reducing discrepancies in the onboarding process, you also make it easier to ensure that every individual is developing in a way that aligns with the company's expectations and values. As a result, employees feel more secure knowing that there is a reliable and fair system in place for their growth. This is a great recruiting benefit for the talent acquisition team as well!

Eases Transfer of Skills

The manager playbook aids in a more efficient transfer of skills and knowledge. A well-structured guide allows managers to navigate the complexities of training employees on both technical skills and company culture. This is especially important for reducing the time it takes for new employees to become fully productive when they enter the performing phase. By providing a clear framework, the playbook helps employees ramp up more quickly, accelerating their contribution to the team and the organization.

Boosts Manager Confidence

With a comprehensive playbook in hand, managers are better equipped with the tools, best practices, and strategies needed to handle various challenges that arise during the onboarding process. This structured approach minimizes uncertainty and enhances the manager's ability to support their new employees. In turn, confident managers foster an environment in which new employees feel at ease with their decision to join the team.

Sets Clear Expectations

The manager playbook allows you to set clear expectations around employee autonomy. Lay out milestones and development goals to ensure that managers and employees are aligned on the path from leg 1 (onboarding) to leg 3 (refinement) of the everboarding relay. This clarity helps managers track progress and determine when an employee is ready to take on more responsibility independently. Having such well-defined metrics not only promotes accountability but also encourages managers to take an active role in their employee's development, which in turn drives faster achievement of autonomy.

Drives Employee Engagement

When new hires are coached by well-prepared managers, they tend to be more engaged and motivated. Feeling supported during their early days in the company helps new employees build confidence, trust in leadership, and a strong connection to the company's mission and goals. By outlining the development process in the manager playbook, you can ensure that new employees are not just passive participants but active learners, creating a culture of growth and continuous improvement.

Helps With Scalability

As companies grow and hire across different roles, departments, and regions, it can be challenging to maintain a high level of development consistency. The manager playbook provides a standardized framework that can be easily adapted to various positions and team dynamics. This makes it easier to scale onboarding and coaching processes without overburdening individual managers.

Makes Data-Driven Improvements Possible

The manager playbook enables your talent development teams to make data-driven improvements. With a structured approach, it becomes easier to track and measure key outcomes, such as time to productivity, retention rates, and employee satisfaction. You can then use this data to continuously refine and optimize the onboarding and coaching processes, ensuring they stay relevant and effective as the company evolves.

Take the Lead in Creating Alignment

This chapter debunked the myth that everboarding is just a replacement for performance management. It also emphasized the unique role everboarding plays in redefining the talent development team's influence. When we are focusing on aligning with broader organizational goals through a powerful partnership with managers, we are also enhancing the new-hire experience. By shifting from a reactive to a proactive role, the talent development team becomes a strategic partner to managers, equipping them with the tools to evaluate and support new hires more effectively, long-term.

CHAPTER 9
Equipping Managers for Ongoing Support

Everboarding Myth #9
Only Fortune 500 companies can pull everboarding off.

It's easy to believe that only massive organizations with unlimited resources can implement an effective everboarding strategy, but that's far from the truth. In fact, this approach is designed to work in organizations of any size because it relies more on intentional systems and consistent practices than budget or headcount.

The third leg of the everboarding relay—refinement—is fast approaching. When a new employee nears the end of the development phase, their manager starts to spend less time with them and they start asking fewer questions. What does this transition look like moving forward? The manager and your talent development team aren't quite finished, but all the work you've put in up front will make this phase feel like the fun part of your job because you'll make an ongoing impact without doing any heavy lifting.

One of the best ways you can continue to support managers and their employees is putting great systems in place. Your team is at the helm of these systems because you're the best group for the job. Everyone expects the talent development team to onboard new people, support managers, and send out assessments and surveys to measure a job well done. What happens after that is different for every organization. I'm here to tell you that this is really where you shine. This is where you show that the value of your team extends well beyond formal training and assessments. You add value by creating systems that sustain performance—and in this chapter, we explore performance management and feedback loops, targeted learning resources, mentoring and coaching, and succession and talent pools.

Performance Management Support

Performance management plays a pivotal role in your everboarding strategy, especially as employees start to take responsibility for their own growth while receiving structured support from their managers and your team. Integrating performance management in a systematic way ensures that employees are continuously developing in alignment with business objectives. This avoids the feedback you never want to hear: "They don't have time for training. They just need to put their heads down and work."

Here's how your talent development team can support frontline managers in employee performance management as everyone transitions to the next leg of the everboarding relay to create a more engaging and growth-focused experience:

- **Cascading goals.** Support managers in linking individual goals to team and company-wide goals. This ensures that every employee understands how their work contributes to larger organizational priorities, helping them stay motivated and aligned. Cascading goals are crucial for every single team in the organization and provide so much clarity and accountability to the company's purpose and mission.
- **Regular goal revisions.** Provide a framework for reviewing and updating goals regularly. As business needs change or employees progress in their development, goals may need to be adjusted to stay relevant. At minimum, review goals halfway through the year, but monthly is ideal. As we all learned in 2020, the world can change quickly, and so can our businesses.
- **Real-time feedback tools.** Implement tools, such as internal feedback platforms, that allow employees and managers to

exchange real-time feedback on specific projects or behaviors. This prevents annual reviews from becoming overwhelming and provides more consistent, actionable feedback.
- **Feedforward.** Train managers on how to provide "feedforward" instead of focusing solely on past performance. *Feedforward* is a forward-looking approach that managers can use to guide employees on how they can improve or expand their skills for future tasks or roles. As Aaron Brown, an insights analyst at Quantum Workplace, has told me, "Even before you start to give feedback, have a precursor conversation about how [your employees] experience feedback. They come to the conversation with prior experiences with getting feedback; oftentimes, it's negative. You still give them the feedback they need; you just change your approach with it."
- **Employee engagement surveys.** Conduct regular engagement surveys to gauge what employees think about the performance management process and how supported they feel in their development. Use this feedback to improve the system.
- **Development progress reviews.** Provide managers with frameworks to help employees reflect on their development and learning journey, offering tools or coaching tips for managers to assist employees with tracking their self-led growth. It may sound simple, but it is also powerful. Seeing their progress has a much different impact than hearing about it. Your LMS or performance management tool should have reports on courses completed, skills or competencies acquired, feedback from managers and peers, and progress on development goals.

Pro Tip

Create scorecards that rate the employee's development in key areas over time, which managers can review during one-on-ones and performance reviews.

One way to track how performance management efforts—and other employee development systems—are working is to have a regular manager–talent development team touchpoint going forward. You should establish structured check-ins between managers and your team to assess their employee's progress. These touchpoints can coincide with existing performance review cycles or quarterly goals, and ensure your team is aware of individual performance and able to provide resources or interventions.

Have a structure that includes a cadence and a clear agenda. One of my favorite reminders for teams is "no agenda, no attenda." Here is an example of what an agenda could include:

1. Employee progress updates (skills growth, training completed, and performance against goals)
2. Identification of development gaps or challenges
3. Support needed from your team (such as new learning materials, workshops, or mentorship opportunities)
4. Career trajectory discussion (to ensure progress is aligned with succession planning or leadership development pathways)

Targeted Learning Resources

Build on the learning journeys that you established earlier with employees and managers. You can update them by creating curated development pathways aligned with both succession plans and documented individual career aspirations. Your team can use a content library (including webinars, courses, and books) that aligns with the employee's long-term goals and the organization's talent strategy. Analyze which skills need to be added or updated as you have more of these discussions.

In the world of higher education, stackable learning is becoming increasingly popular for supporting adults with full-time jobs. You can implement similar style of learning in your organization. Stackable learning is like microlearning, but instead of consuming small bits of information over time, it is focused on employees achieving skills that build on one another to obtain a larger competency, such as a degree or certification. Imagine if you offered employees something similar.

There is a demand within our businesses to keep up with external factors, but employees are often already looking outside the organization for solutions. Seek out partnerships with universities, digital learning companies, and industry experts to bring their external knowledge to your employees. Can you co-create stackable learning content to elevate skills that your organization desperately needs? The possibilities are endless; you just need to identify them.

Mentoring and Coaching

While the employee is carrying their own baton, your team can use the established new-hire mentoring program that involves employees sharing knowledge and fostering a culture of continuous growth to develop another program to support them. Use elements you have already created, such as a mentor application process, to design a program that meets employees' needs as they progress in their development. The mentor also benefits from this peer interaction because they gain leadership experience while also learning something from the newer employee's experience.

Create a framework for pairing employees with mentors who can guide their development. This could include regular check-ins, goal-setting sessions, and resource sharing. Also provide mentors with feedback training and access to coaching modules to ensure there is proper communication between peers. The last thing you want to worry about is a misunderstanding from well-intended advice.

Another option is to create more informal 360-degree feedback and coaching opportunities. Peer feedback adds an additional layer of insight and perspective, fostering a culture of shared growth. There are two ways you can incorporate feedback loops:

- **Feedback circles.** The talent development team can facilitate peer feedback sessions for employees to share insights on one another's performance and development. A team lead or other senior employee could also lead this discussion.
- **Cross-training and collaboration.** Encourage peer learning by having employees mentor one another or collaborate on

projects, and use feedback loops to reflect on these experiences, fostering a collaborative learning environment.

Succession and Talent Pool Integration

Are talent development and talent management integrated at your organization? Your answer truly matters in this phase. You've done so much to help employees begin performing independently, but there are many other people and teams that affect their future that you must align with too. Have you considered them? Integrating these elements into the system ensures that employees in the refinement phase are not only focused on their current roles but are also preparing for future opportunities that align with organizational goals.

Here's an example of how you can systematically work with managers to support succession planning and other talent management efforts as employees transition to the refinement phase.

Succession planning:
- *Key competencies identification.* Work with leadership and managers to identify the key competencies and skills required for critical roles within the organization. These competencies should be tied to the organization's long-term strategy and future needs.
- *Alignment with talent development efforts.* Work with managers to create personalized development plans for employees, focusing on identified competencies. For example, if the organization is growing in digital transformation, ensure employees on a leadership track are developing digital fluency.
- *Stretch assignments.* Provide opportunities for employees to gain experience in areas outside their current role. These assignments should expose them to cross-functional work, new challenges, or leadership responsibilities that align with the future roles they're being groomed for.
- *Readiness indicators.* Regularly discuss with managers which employees have shown potential for future leadership or key

roles. Your team can provide insights on training completion, development growth, and readiness for new responsibilities. Develop metrics or indicators that reflect an employee's readiness for succession. This could include performance evaluations, leadership potential assessments, or project-based feedback. You can also use technology dashboards to track employees in the succession pipeline. Regularly update leadership on these employees' progress and how they are advancing in their development.

Engagement and retention strategies:
- *Career progression clarity.* Clearly outline the steps employees can take to move through talent pools. Transparency helps manage expectations and keeps high-potential employees engaged by providing a clear path forward.
- *High-visibility projects.* Assign talent pool members to high-visibility or high-impact projects, which will allow them to demonstrate their capabilities to leadership. This provides critical experience and keeps them motivated by contributing meaningfully to the organization's goals.
- *Regular check-ins.* Have regular, structured check-ins between the talent development team, managers, and talent pool members to review progress, adjust development plans, and ensure alignment with career aspirations and organizational needs.

Tailored development programs:
- *Leadership development programs.* For employees in the leadership talent pool, create structured leadership development programs that include mentorship, formal training, executive coaching, and exposure to strategic decision-making processes.
- *Technical expertise programs.* For those in technical or specialized roles, create learning tracks that allow employees to deepen their expertise and develop leadership skills relevant to their function. For example, a top software engineer might take on a project leadership role in addition to technical training.

- *Blended learning.* Combine different types of learning resources (such as online courses, mentorship, and on-the-job training) tailored to the needs of each talent pool.

Strategy Over Spend

In this chapter, we tackled one of the biggest myths about everboarding: that only large organizations can successfully implement it. The truth is, everboarding is scalable for any company because it's built on intentional systems rather than deep pockets. Meaning, the success of everboarding doesn't depend on having a huge budget or an abundance of resources.

We explored how performance management, targeted learning resources, mentoring and coaching, and succession planning play critical roles in sustaining employee growth beyond the onboarding and development phases. By equipping managers with structured tools, you ensure they have the support they need to guide employees toward continuous success. I also introduced the power of stackable learning, peer mentoring, and feedback loops to create an ecosystem in which employees take ownership of their growth while still being supported.

Ultimately, everboarding doesn't just benefit employees—it also strengthens managers and aligns with business objectives to reinforce the strategic value of talent development. As we transition into the final phase of the everboarding relay, it's clear that the role of talent development doesn't end when onboarding does.

In this part of the book, we identified and worked through ways to engage managers and align them with new-hire development efforts. Managers are your lifeline to onboarding's learning reinforcement, skill application, and overall new-hire success. We began by easing managers into this change with the MOCCA Change Management Methodology to support their embrace of the everboarding strategy. We then addressed the need to enable managers with people development skills through the personal trainer method and the manager toolkit to remove frustration from administrative tasks. Then, we identified the risks of recency bias and other progress assessment pitfalls that occur in new-hire experiences with their manager and how to navigate them. Last, we discussed ongoing performance management and its role in succession planning to create a sustainable talent pool. In the next part, we'll step into the self-led employee development phase in which the new hire is ready to accept the baton and own their further development.

Part 3
Employee-Led Refinement

CHAPTER 10
Creating an Environment for Self-Led Learning

Everboarding Myth #10
Everboarding requires you to create many one-time training events.

In our modern world, staying stagnant is not an option—either for organizations or individuals. Traditional learning models that rely heavily on structured, one-time onboarding processes are rapidly becoming obsolete, which in turn is making your team obsolete! Instead, the focus has shifted toward creating environments where employees are encouraged to continue learning throughout their careers to perform at new levels of expectations.

This chapter's opening myth often stems from a misunderstanding of what everboarding is. It's not about overloading your team with endless training sessions or trying to squeeze every ounce of knowledge into formal, one-time events. Instead, it's about cultivating an ecosystem where learning is ongoing, organic, and aligned with each employee's personal and professional growth goals. By moving away from one-off programs and focusing on enabling self-led learning, you reduce the need for constant event planning while empowering employees to take the reins of their development.

Your goal is to foster a culture of growth through self-led exploration, curiosity, and ownership that's not just led by the talent development team or managers. In the future workplace, the most successful employees won't be the ones who wait for training to be handed to them. They'll be the ones who actively seek out knowledge, experiment with new skills, and apply that knowledge and those skills in real-time. So, how do you create an environment where continuous self-led learning becomes second nature? How do you make learning a habit in your organization?

Nudge Theory: Gentle Pushes Toward Growth

One of the foundational aspects of cultivating a growth culture is using *nudge theory*. This psychological concept involves subtly guiding individuals toward desirable behaviors without forcing them (Thaler and Sunstein 2008). While nudge theory isn't a new idea, it became a common topic of conversation in the business world in 2008 when professionals realized it was much more than a marketing tool. Nudge theory, simply put, is choice architecture and suggests that we can strongly influence an individual's choices with the right messaging and narrowed options. Within talent development, the goal isn't to mandate learning but to encourage it through well-timed suggestions and opportunities. This requires the use of technology, including AI, but it's also very human powered.

For example, if an employee has expressed interest in moving into a leadership role and wants to improve their leadership skills, a gentle nudge could be sending them relevant articles, inviting them to leadership webinars, or suggesting they shadow a manager. You can embed these nudges into daily workflows so they feel organic and integrated rather than like an external demand. When you personalize nudges based on individual goals and career aspirations, they become even more powerful. Table 10-1 shows an example of nudge theory in action.

Cross-Role Exposure

Continuous learning thrives in environments where employees are exposed to different aspects of the business, not just their day-to-day tasks. Traditionally, departments have worked in silos with employees becoming specialists in one area—but this limits their growth potential and critical thinking skills. Encouraging employees to explore roles outside their primary function broadens their understanding of the business and develops versatile skill sets.

Table 10-1.
Nudge Theory Application Example

Stage	Employee Behavior	Friction Point	Nudge Intervention	Desired Outcome
Resistance	Hesitant to switch; worried about disruption	Fear of losing productivity due to existing workflows	• Identify key pain points. • Acknowledge concerns.	Employees feel heard and less defensive.
Awareness and familiarity	Skeptical about benefits	Uncertain if the new system can match their existing setup	• Demonstrate feature parity. • Show side-by-side workflow replication.	Employees recognize similarities and see potential benefits.
Enablement and support	Struggling with transition	Complexity in setting up new automations and integrations	• Preconfigured workflows • Automation duplication	Users see immediate functionality with minimal effort.
Adoption and reinforcement	Reluctant to engage fully	Lack of motivation to invest time in learning	• Gamify adoption. • Celebrate early adopters.	More employees start using the new tool.
Sustained behavior change	Using the new tool, but may revert back to old habits	Old habits and lack of continued engagement	• Provide ongoing training. • Showcase time-saving benefits.	There's long-term adoption and improved efficiency.

Consider a tenured sales employee who believes that management has to be the next step in their career; however, they've also realized that coaching isn't where their true strengths lie. Instead of confining their growth to a linear career path, why not offer them the chance to shadow a sales engineer for a week or collaborate with the operations team on a cross-functional project? By exposing employees to different roles, you can offer a range of learning opportunities and help them see the broader context of their work.

Cross-role exposure also encourages empathy between departments. When an employee understands another role's challenges and workflows, they are better equipped to collaborate effectively and think holistically. They acquire a higher level of business acumen once they're exposed to business processes outside their role.

This is a cornerstone of creating agile, cross-functional teams—something that is increasingly valuable in today's collaborative, lean, project-based work environment.

Knowledge Sharing and Legacy Knowledge

In many organizations, knowledge remains locked in silos—whether in a SME's mind or across different departments. Creating a culture that doesn't just encourage knowledge sharing but also ingrains it into daily routines is essential for self-led learning.

A great way to facilitate knowledge sharing is through mentorship programs, communities of practice, and collaborative platforms where employees can exchange insights and resources. When knowledge flows freely, employees gain access to diverse perspectives and expertise.

This goes beyond formal training sessions. For example, you could create a lunch & learn series for employees from different departments to share their expertise or develop internal blogs and discussion forums for people to contribute and interact with useful content.

Aaron Brown, an insights analyst at Quantum Workplace, told me that he likes to ask, "Who is the one person that knows the why behind many of the things at your organization?" That person has probably been with you for 14 years or more, and the only place to access that information is from their brain. Take time to get that knowledge and make it available.

By promoting a culture that values open knowledge sharing, you not only foster learning but also help employees build relationships that support their professional growth. This continuous access to internal expertise makes learning a dynamic, interactive process rather than something confined to structured training sessions.

Knowledge and Resource Curation

In the digital age, the availability of learning resources can be overwhelming. Employees are constantly bombarded with articles, videos, podcasts, and training programs. However, without proper guidance, it's easy for this wealth of information to become background noise. Curating the resources within your everboarding strategy ensures that you share only the most relevant content instead of asking employees to sift through unnecessary content and waste valuable time. It also makes learning more digestible and timely and helps them avoid burnout from consumption.

You can partner with managers to curate learning paths tailored to their team's needs and career stages. Think of it as creating a resource library that employees can access at any time, with content curated specifically for their roles, goals, and development paths. Curated learning paths allow employees to take control of their own development, accessing the right information when it's needed, without feeling lost in a sea of content.

Curated knowledge also encourages deeper engagement with learning materials. Instead of passively consuming content, employees should be encouraged to reflect on how they can apply what they've learned in real situations. For instance, after completing a learning module, they could write a reflection piece or discuss key takeaways with their manager or peers. This process helps solidify learning and keeps it relevant to their current work.

Remember when we discussed personalizing learning journeys in chapter 3? Managers have to be involved in building the road map alongside the talent development team. They can become curators of learning opportunities, offering relevant content and experiences that can gently push employees in the right direction. Not all coaching from a manager requires them to provide the employee with answers. In many cases, they just need to connect their employees to answers and new experiences. This alleviates pressure from the manager and diversifies the organization's future leaders with thoughts and ideas that aren't cyclical.

When I was consulting with Spekit, I worked with learning leaders in various industries to implement their onboarding and other learning programs. A common piece I helped them implement was a learning playlist. The playlist captures external (or internal) resources—such as books, podcast episodes, articles, people to follow, and associations to follow or join—that a leader wants their team to consume.

You can make your learning playlist a single document to reference, or take it a step further and use the resources individually to create a drip campaign. During onboarding, you could send a weekly communication that highlights an item on the list and key takeaways. Managers could also pull from it when they're stuck and don't know what to suggest to an employee who's working on a new skill.

Lindsay Hoyle, a senior enablement manager at Smartsheet, is an advocate for using learning playlists because of the immense value they provide. During her time at Stripe, her team offered learning playlists for their startup and small to medium business organizations to use in their onboarding and continued development programs. They included what employees needed to know about the typical industries and roles they'd be speaking to at other companies. Stripe partnered with their venture capitalists (VCs)—who fed Stripe some of their startup leads—to curate materials that would better support this team and prepare them to speak to founders and executives at smaller organizations. This gave the VCs confidence in putting sellers in front of companies, insight into what it was like to work at a smaller business, and helped them speak the same language.

Focused Learning Paths

Just as someone's career journey should not be linear, neither should their learning journey. One-size-fits-all learning programs often miss the mark because they fail to address individual needs. Every employee has unique strengths, challenges, and career aspirations. Thus, focused and personalized learning paths are essential.

Leaders should focus on identifying specific growth areas for each employee through feedback, performance reviews, and self-assessments. With this understanding, tailored learning paths can be developed that guide employees toward their personal and professional goals. These paths should be flexible, allowing employees to pursue learning at their own pace, while still being supported by ongoing feedback from peers and mentors.

In addition to technical skills, these paths should incorporate soft skills such as leadership, communication, and emotional intelligence. A comprehensive, personalized approach to learning ensures that employees not only become better at their jobs but also evolve as well-rounded professionals who are prepared for future challenges.

FAQ Channels

In the everboarding framework, particularly in hybrid or remote teams, maintaining consistency in communication and knowledge sharing can be challenging. An FAQ (frequently asked questions) channel ensures that all employees—regardless of location—have access to the same standardized, up-to-date information. This consistency helps prevent misinformation or discrepancies in how policies, processes, or tools are understood across the organization.

An updated FAQ channel ensures that all employees stay aligned with organizational objectives and procedures. This is crucial for maintaining a smooth everboarding process, especially as employees move from onboarding to the development and refinement phases. The FAQ channel becomes a living resource that grows with the organization, helping your employees stay informed and up to date without requiring formal training sessions.

In the refinement phase, maintaining FAQ channels encourages autonomy and self-reliance, enabling employees to troubleshoot and find solutions independently. It reduces dependency on direct support and allows them to take control of their individual performance.

FAQs are difficult to capture. Many questions happen in the flow of work, so employees are directed to a person who is simply solving the problem and moving on. There is no one way to capture this information. In fact, there are many ways in which you can attempt to gather and organize them. It's easy to write FAQs for new pieces of technology, but it's not as easy to identify a company's history, release notes, custom ordering processes, and where something lives.

As employees move from onboarding to development and ultimately to the refinement phase, the challenges they face and the questions they have will evolve. An FAQ channel can address these changing needs by offering role-specific information that supports each phase. For instance, early in the onboarding phase, FAQs might focus on company policies and tools, whereas in the refinement phase, they might address leadership development, career progression, or advanced problem-solving techniques.

FAQ channels help reduce the burden on managers and team leaders, who would otherwise need to answer routine questions repeatedly. This frees up their time to focus on higher-level development and coaching because employees can help themselves more easily. In your everboarding strategy, you are asking managers to play a key role in guiding employees through the development phase. Maintaining FAQ channels allows them to do this more deeply.

A Culture of Learning Is the Foundation of a Culture of Growth

This chapter debunked the myth that everboarding requires numerous one-time training events by shifting the focus from structured, scheduled learning to an ecosystem of continuous self-led development. Instead of overloading employees with isolated training sessions, everboarding fosters an environment where learning happens naturally with exposure to new experiences. Creating an environment of continuous self-led learning requires intentional design. From gentle nudges to cross-role exposure, knowledge sharing, curation, and personalized learning paths, these strategies collectively foster a culture where employees take ownership of their growth. As a result, organizations will have agile, adaptable teams ready to meet the challenges of tomorrow.

By shifting away from linear career paths and embracing a more dynamic, cyclical approach to learning, organizations empower employees to continuously evolve. In the end, it's not just about onboarding—it's about everboarding.

CHAPTER 11
Recognizing Continuous Growth

Everboarding Myth #11
It's the same as employee engagement.

One of the most persistent myths about everboarding is that it's simply another term for employee engagement. While everboarding and engagement are related, they are far from synonymous. Engagement focuses on how connected and committed employees feel to their work and the organization, while everboarding is about enabling continuous learning, growth, and refinement throughout the employee life cycle. Engagement can be a byproduct of everboarding, but the core of everboarding lies in the structured development opportunities it provides to employees at every stage of their journey.

Recognition plays a pivotal role in breaking this myth. A robust recognition system acknowledges employees not just for their engagement, but for their ongoing growth and contributions. It reflects the essence of everboarding: Employees are never finished learning or growing. By celebrating both small wins and major achievements, recognition reinforces desired behaviors, motivates continuous improvement, and strengthens the bond between the employee and the organization.

During the refinement phase, formal recognition helps sustain motivation by celebrating milestones in an employee's development, further strengthening their commitment to personal growth and the company. It supports a culture in which employees take pride in their work and feel valued as they refine their skills. Growth happens when we reinforce desired skills and behaviors. In this chapter, we cover some different ways to recognize employee development and the steps to establish a recognition system.

Types of Recognition

Not all employees love public recognition, so it's important to understand their personal preferences. Additionally, it can be used as a comparison tool—be consistent when giving recognition to your team. Employees notice what does and doesn't get recognized, which can lead to unintended feelings of inadequacy. You need to establish guidelines for giving recognition. Here are some forms of recognition you can incorporate:

- **Performance-based recognition** can be tied to specific milestones, goals, or metrics an employee meets as part of their role. For instance, you can celebrate when they meet sales targets, complete projects, or hit KPIs.
- **Peer recognition.** Systems that encourage colleagues to recognize one another's contributions can foster a collaborative environment. You might implement this through platforms where peers can shout out or nominate one another for certain awards.
- **Manager-driven recognition** is critical in the refinement phase. It could include quarterly awards, performance reviews with a strong focus on celebrating improvements, or public recognition during team meetings.
- **Cultural contribution awards.** Beyond performance, recognizing employees who embody company values and contribute to the organization's culture (including mentorship, innovation, or inclusion) can enhance engagement.
- **Skill mastery and learning.** Employees in the refinement phase are often deepening their expertise. A formal recognition system that highlights the completion of certifications, learning programs, or mastery of new skills can be a powerful motivator.

Because many organizations continue to operate with hybrid and remote teams, you may have to be more intentional and provide a more unique experience for employees who are distributed away from headquarters. Their view into the organization is more limited, so consider adding three elements to make them feel included and help them embrace recognition as proudly as they would in person:

1. **Equitable visibility.** Ensure that remote and in-office employees are equally considered in recognition efforts. You could use virtual platforms to host recognition events or ensure that award announcements are made in both virtual and in-person formats.
2. **Celebrate contributions publicly.** In hybrid environments, remote workers might feel less visible. Publicly celebrating achievements via company-wide emails, digital bulletins, or virtual town halls ensures everyone feels like part of the company culture, no matter where they work.
3. **Use data to track recognition.** Track how often individuals or teams (remote and in-office) are being recognized and adjust where necessary to maintain a balance and avoid bias.

Establish a Formal Recognition System

Growth will stall without a recognition system, but establishing one involves a culture and behavior change that requires careful planning. However, the entire company can benefit from a feeling of cohesion. Here are 10 steps you can take to establish a formal recognition system:

1. **Define objectives and outcomes.** Before creating a system, clarify why recognition is important and what outcomes you aim to achieve.
2. **Identify what to recognize.** Recognize actions and achievements that align with the organization's values and contribute to its success, such as performance, cultural contributions, skill attainment, and innovation.
3. **Establish clear and transparent criteria.** Create guidelines on what merits recognition so employees understand how to earn it;

for example, performance benchmarks, behavioral expectations, learning, and development.
4. **Choose recognition methods.** Decide how to recognize employees, balancing formal and informal methods.
5. **Set up recognition platforms and tools.** Choose tools and platforms that streamline recognition and ensure visibility across the organization. Don't forget to integrate them with your communication tools like Slack and Teams.
6. **Train managers and employees.** Educate managers and employees on the importance of recognition and how to effectively implement the system. Note that you must train managers before employees. If possible, also include team leads and supervisors in the manager training. However, managers should never be learning alongside their employees if you want early adoption.
7. **Launch the recognition system.** Formally launch the system with a company-wide announcement to set expectations and excitement. Include these elements in your launch:
    - *Kickoff event.* Hold a launch event (virtually or in-person) for leaders to explain the system, its importance, and how it works. Offer initial awards to set the tone.
    - *Communication strategy.* Send out clear guidelines via email, the intranet, or a company meeting on how recognition will be given and the criteria for earning it.
    - *FAQs and support.* Provide information and resources so employees can easily understand the process. Offer ongoing support for managers and employees who have questions about the system.
8. **Monitor, evaluate, and adjust.** Track the recognition system's effectiveness and be open to making adjustments.
9. **Celebrate and publicize successes.** Keep the momentum going by regularly celebrating achievements.
10. **Embed recognition into company culture.** Ensure that recognition becomes an integral part of your company culture, not just a program.

Ideas for Taking Action

Todd Pernicek and Aaron Brown, insights analysts at Quantum Workplace (a human resources technology company that specializes in employee engagement and performance), are no strangers to recognition and the impact it has on organizations. I asked them for some of their best ideas for making recognition work. Here's what they had to say:

First, don't rely only on the formal aspects of your recognition program. As Aaron tells me, "Your formal recognition program cannot be your only form of recognition. It has to be a component of the entire recognition philosophy in your organization." This involves getting people to buy in to the idea that recognition happens in many different ways, and you can't just limit yourself to one.

"Formal recognition scares a lot of people because it can be intimidating," Aaron adds. "For instance, I see employees talk themselves out of giving recognition because they compare how they write up recognition to how someone else does and think they can't compete." That means employees worthy of recognition for their continuous growth may get lost in the shuffle, which could lead to discouragement and possibly to exiting your company.

Once you get past the formal recognition, tenure awards, and service anniversary dates, it's between the manager and employee. Talent development should work with people managers to realize that appreciating and acknowledging employees for their development can happen within your formal recognition system—and organically in the course of day-to-day operations.

Second, if you're relying on a formal recognition system, communicate clearly and transparently to everyone in the organization how it works. You don't want an opaque recognition system to cause resentment and blowback on your organizational culture. Todd Pernicek says, "Just like feedback, recognition can go wrong so quickly. Everyone is getting recognized except this person, this team, or this department. It can have unintended dire consequences to engagement and culture."

So, with a recognition system, ask yourself, what are you hoping to enable and why? "Make sure that with any system you use, that you are deliberate around how you're going to enable it," Todd continues. "Make sure people know how to use it and consider incentivizing recognition to drive the desired behaviors. This can be a points accrual system behind the scenes or gamified for everyone to see."

Recognition's Integral Role in Everboarding

The chapter illustrated that engagement may result from everboarding, but it is not the core of the concept. Instead, the core of everboarding lies in providing structured development opportunities that encourage ongoing skill building and personal growth throughout an employee's life cycle. Recognition acknowledges employees for their development and achievements, motivating them to keep learning and refining their skills, rather than merely rewarding them for engagement with the company. Recognition isn't a one-size-fits-all solution. As employees move through different phases of their career, the type and focus of recognition should adapt to their evolving needs and roles. Recognition during everboarding reflects this life cycle, ensuring it remains relevant and motivating.

1. **Onboarding.** During the onboarding phase, recognition helps new employees feel welcomed and appreciated as they adjust to their roles. At this stage, recognition might focus on small wins—quick integration into team dynamics, early project successes, or hitting initial learning milestones. This reinforces the sense that the employee is on the right track and has the company's support.
2. **Development.** As the employee moves into the development phase, with the manager playing a pivotal role, recognition should shift to focus on skill mastery, performance achievements, and contributions to team success. Managers can use recognition as a tool to guide employees through learning and growth opportunities, supporting continuous engagement and personal development.
3. **Refinement.** In the refinement phase, employees are more autonomous, taking charge of their own growth and career trajectory. Recognition in this phase should be more personalized,

acknowledging not just performance, but also leadership, innovation, mentorship, and the employee's broader contribution to company culture. It's at this stage that recognition becomes crucial in helping employees feel valued for their long-term contributions and maintaining their engagement over time. Recognition for ongoing development—such as taking on new challenges, mentoring others, or leading change—keeps them motivated to continue growing even after they've reached a level of expertise.

Recognition is not an optional add-on but another system to support your everboarding strategy. It supports the entire journey from onboarding to the refinement phase by continually reinforcing behaviors and achievements that align with personal growth and organizational success. A recognition system that evolves with the employee's development keeps them engaged, drives continuous learning, and ultimately leads to higher retention and organizational performance. This last phase, in particular, shifts from performance-based rewards to acknowledging deeper contributions like leadership, innovation, and mentorship—ensuring that employees remain invested in their growth and the success of the company.

CHAPTER 12
Bringing in Current Employees

Everboarding Myth #12
It's only for new employees.

The first time I shared my everboarding strategy with a client, they said to me, "I love this, but how do you get current employees on board with it?" They were going through what many other companies experience: Employees were burnt out and just wanted to be left alone. When an everboarding strategy is done right, no one thinks, "Great, now we have to do this everboarding thing too." Everboarding shouldn't feel like "one more thing." It's not a burden or a distraction; instead, it's a seamless part of an employee's day that enhances their experience and makes work easier and more fulfilling.

As we approach the final chapter in this journey through the refinement phase of everboarding, it's critical to focus on current employees who are the backbone of any organization. Unlike new hires, these individuals already have established habits, routines, and expectations. Successfully integrating them into an everboarding strategy often requires an additional layer of intentionality.

Start with addressing potential barriers like change fatigue and ensuring managers are equipped to lead the charge. If structured development is new to your organization, you'll also need to introduce foundational elements like performance feedback and personalized learning paths to create a solid framework for success. For current employees, these tools show that growth isn't just a requirement for new hires; it's an opportunity for everyone to continuously improve.

And so, this chapter explores how to bring current employees into the fold, manage change fatigue, and harness the potential of artificial intelligence (AI) to enhance the employee experience.

Where to Start

If you're implementing an everboarding strategy, your tenured employees will have missed out on new experiences, but that doesn't mean you should ignore them. Start by getting their input. What do they need right now to advance their development? Include their voice when deciding how you'll move forward.

The development phase is a great place to start for inspiration. However, current employees are already in the refinement phase of everboarding. So, consider using a well-structured survey, which can provide valuable insights into how employees feel about their current roles, their readiness for change, and their development needs. This feedback can help ensure that the initiatives in the refinement phase are targeted and effective.

Think of this task like benchmarking employees for skills. Understand the gaps at an individual, team, and business function level. Here is an example of a survey I used with a client, Data Axle (see their complete case study in the appendix). You don't have to use all these questions, but doing so ensures you have very little left to uncover.

Current role satisfaction:
- *Job satisfaction.* How satisfied are you with your current role and responsibilities?
- *Role clarity.* Do you think that your role is clearly defined? Do you understand your expectations?
- *Skills utilization.* Do you think that you are able to fully use your skills and abilities in your current role?

Development opportunities:
- *Learning and growth.* Are there adequate opportunities for learning and growth in your current position?

- *Development support.* Do you feel supported by your manager and the organization in pursuing development opportunities?
- *Access to resources.* Do you have access to the necessary tools, training, and resources to help you develop in your role?

Change readiness and fatigue:
- *Change communication.* How well does the organization communicate upcoming changes that may affect your role or department?
- *Change fatigue.* Do you feel overwhelmed by the number of changes or initiatives being implemented?
- *Change impact.* How do you think the changes in the organization have affected your job satisfaction and performance?

Feedback and participation:
- *Feedback mechanisms.* Do you think your feedback is heard and acted on by leadership?
- *Collaboration.* Are there sufficient opportunities for you to collaborate with your peers and share ideas or challenges?
- *Peer learning.* How valuable do you find mentoring or knowledge-sharing programs within the company?

Use of technology and AI:
- *Tech tools.* Do you feel confident using the current technology and tools provided by the organization?
- *AI and automation.* How comfortable are you with the introduction of AI and automation in your daily tasks?
- *Tech training needs.* Are there any specific areas where you would like more training or support regarding AI or new technology?

Well-being and work-life balance:
- *Workload management.* Do you think that your workload is manageable within regular working hours?
- *Support for well-being.* Does the company provide adequate support for mental and physical well-being?
- *Work-life balance.* How would you rate your work-life balance, and do you think the organization supports maintaining it?

Future aspirations:
- *Career goals.* Are your long-term career goals being discussed and incorporated into your development plan?
- *Succession planning.* Do you think that there is a clear path for advancement or transition into different roles within the company?

> **Pro Tip**
>
> Communicate the results of the survey transparently. Anytime you survey employees to this degree, you should share the results to ensure everyone feels heard.

Bringing Current Employees Into the Fold

To effectively integrate current employees into the everboarding process, you have to start with two major initiatives—celebrating milestones and creating personalized development plans—as well as the reasons behind them. I strongly believe this information needs to come from their direct leader and the other respective senior leaders within their team to demonstrate support for the long haul. You want leaders to send the message "I care about your development" instead of "I was told to care about your development."

Celebrating Milestones

Acknowledging the achievements of new employees throughout the refinement phase is a must, and your current, tenured employees are no exception. Recognizing milestones, both big and small, reinforces their contributions and keeps them engaged in their development journey.

Not every employee wants to climb the metaphorical ladder. Many of them want to be solid contributors in their current role and continue to excel in it. Find other ways to recognize them that aren't promotions or a new certification. It could be mentorship or a project outside the team. Managers must look for moments in which the employee enriches the team's culture.

I once had a sales leader, Adam, who did this very well. We called it "think generously." Every month, Adam celebrated a milestone on his team—which he was able to do because he kept track of them. And he was only able to do that because he was purposeful and intentional about discovering them. For example, he had an employee, Patrick, who had been with the company longer than him (12 years) and he had stayed in that same role. Patrick's title changed as the company evolved, but his role didn't shift much. Adam was Patrick's new leader because of restructuring. (Everyone knew Patrick could produce so every leader wanted him on their team.)

The monthly recognition call came around, and Adam recognized Patrick for helping test and give feedback on a new tool the company launched. Adam knew that use of technology was not Patrick's strongest skill, and it was outside his comfort zone to use and give feedback on something he'd never used before. Adam also knew how busy Patrick was, and for the first time in years, Patrick had stepped away from his usual role to add value to the organization and his team and still met his performance goals. In the past, Patrick had always declined these requests, but this time, he didn't because he knew his efforts wouldn't go unrecognized by his leader and that Adam would see the value in it when other leaders had not supported it.

Celebrating milestones of all kinds matters. There is immense value in allowing employees to grow in their professional career outside the scope of their work.

Personalized Development Plans

Each employee has unique skills and aspirations. Work collaboratively with managers and employees to develop personalized growth plans that align their goals with the organization's objectives. This not only motivates employees but also reinforces their value within the company. Personalized development plans also help reduce the need for PIPs because they ensure clarity around role expectations.

Your team can work together to help managers establish development plans with their tenured staff. The last thing you want is for managers to catch wind that all the new employees are getting personalized plans and assume the initiative is only for their new hires. Try to get tenured employees on their own plans around the same time as new employees. This turns it into a company-wide priority, rather than just a new-hire training initiative.

Skills Gaps and How to Address Them

Skills gaps are not unique to any organization. We all have them, and we all work tirelessly to solve for them. How we identify, develop, and address training opportunities for our organizations' skills gaps can vary greatly. However, there are simple ways to approach these challenges that are not industry specific.

First, identify the team's business goals and work backward from there. Identify the actions everyone will have to take for the team to meet the goal. Managers can help by assessing their employees' competency and performance to identify what skills they need to develop.

My colleague Jonathan Kvarfordt uses what I believe to be the best steps for skills development:

1. Define key business goals for the team.
2. Identify key accomplishments that fulfill the organization's mission and achieve its goals.
3. Break accomplishments into key behaviors and tasks.
4. Analyze the ecosystem that's needed to enable behaviors and accomplishments.
5. Validate the model with individual employees and their managers.
6. Use the model to design enablers (such as training, tools, incentives, and so on).

For each skill that requires training development, you can apply Kvarfordt's LOPAFT Model—which stands for learn, observe WGLL (what good looks like in the real world), practice, application, feedback, and teach (Figure 12-1). Kvarfordt created this model to address the skills gap epidemic in any industry and organization.

Figure 12-1.
The LOPAFT Model for Skill Training

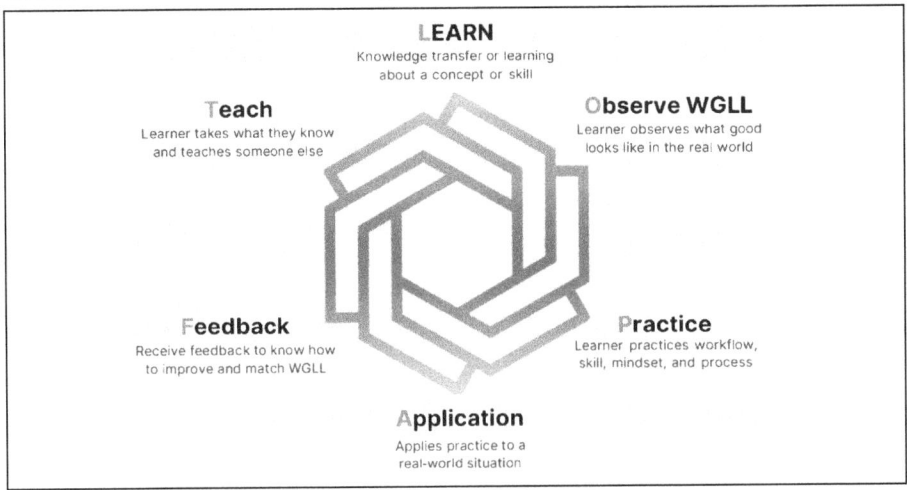

Image courtesy of Jonathan Kvarfordt.

Managing Change Fatigue With AI

Employees have long believed they don't have time to learn new skills as often as they would like. We've all heard those sentiments, but they won't be a problem much longer because AI is transforming how we approach talent management, employee development, and overall organizational growth. In the refinement phase of everboarding, AI plays a crucial role in helping you ensure that your current employees continue to grow, remain engaged, and feel valued. Integrating AI into the talent development ecosystem is not just about automation; it's about enabling faster and more personalized, scalable development solutions. The benefits are endless when using AI responsibly.

One of the most significant contributions AI makes in employee development is the ability to offer personalized learning experiences. As we've discussed throughout this book, traditional one-size-fits-all training programs no longer meet the needs of diverse workforces. AI-driven platforms can change that by tailoring development to each individual's specific needs. You can avoid disrupting their day and instead make learning flow into the work they're already doing. AI can analyze employee performance data, their learning preferences, career aspirations, and even personality traits to design customized learning paths, which can include a mix of online courses, on-the-job challenges, mentoring, and micro-learning modules.

You can make predictions about current (and new) employees to avoid burnout or performance regression. AI can track KPIs over time and identify patterns and anomalies in employee performance. For example, it can detect when an employee's productivity starts to decline, helping managers intervene before issues worsen. Predictive analytics can forecast which employees might be at risk of disengagement or turnover so you can act accordingly.

You also no longer have to rely heavily on surveys because there are tools that can assess factors like employee sentiment, communication frequency, and engagement with company resources. This allows you to better understand the factors that contribute to employee satisfaction with tools and software, as well as help you tailor initiatives to boost morale and retention.

Last, employees can devote more time to cross-team collaboration projects with smarter AI-based project management tools, which can help with task completion, identify patterns to predict potential bottlenecks and suggest ways to improve team productivity. These tools can also automate repetitive tasks, allowing employees to focus on more strategic initiatives.

I want to call attention to the fact that AI doesn't replace the human element in talent development—it enhances it. Human oversight is essential for interpreting AI-generated data, making decisions with empathy, and providing the emotional support that AI cannot. When used effectively, AI tools can support your managers by reducing administrative burdens, allowing them to focus on coaching, mentoring, and fostering deeper connections with their teams.

Integrating Tenured Employees

This chapter debunked the myth that everboarding is only for new employees and supported its relevance for current, tenured staff. Successfully integrating these employees into your everboarding strategy requires intentional efforts to overcome barriers like change fatigue and ensure managers are equipped to lead with empathy and strategy.

Here are some key strategies to remember:
- **Start with feedback.** Gather employee input through structured formal surveys to understand their current development needs and readiness for change. Transparency in sharing results builds trust and makes employees feel heard.
- **Celebrate milestones.** Recognize achievements of all sizes to keep employees engaged and help them see their individual value. Tailor recognition to individual preferences and contributions, fostering a culture of appreciation beyond traditional promotions.
- **Personalize development plans.** Collaborate with employees and managers to create growth plans that align individual aspirations with organizational goals. This aids in reducing skills gaps and increasing overall engagement.
- **Leverage AI for development.** Use AI tools to personalize learning, identify skills gaps, predict burnout, and provide managers with actionable insights. AI can enhance human-led development and save time by creating scalable, tailored solutions that won't overwhelm employees.

When you integrate current employees into the refinement phase of everboarding, you get to create a culture that values growth for everyone. You are blending recognition, development, and innovation into a seamless experience that supports both your retention goals and the organization's productivity goals.

In this part of the book, we identified how to empower employees in the refinement phase—the final stage of everboarding—when employees take full ownership of their development. We started by debunking the myth that everboarding is about continuous one-time training events, and instead determined that it's about establishing an environment for self-led learning through nudge theory, cross-role exposure, and knowledge sharing. We then focused on the importance of recognition as a driver of continuous growth, detailing how structured recognition systems reinforce learning, motivate employees, and strengthen their connection to the organization. Finally, we tackled the challenge of integrating tenured employees into everboarding by addressing change fatigue, personalizing development plans, and leveraging AI to support growth at scale. Next, we'll conclude with actionable key takeaways and case studies of everboarding success.

CONCLUSION
The Everboarding Difference

Everboarding Myth #13
Everboarding is another flavor of the month.
It won't stick.

Let's take a moment to reflect on what we've covered throughout this book and how this new approach can transform your role in talent development. The transition from traditional onboarding to everboarding isn't just a fresh coat of paint; it's a complete renovation of how we think about talent management and employee engagement. So, grab a cup of coffee (or your favorite beverage), and let's dive into the key takeaways that highlight the everboarding difference.

1. Continuous Engagement Is Key
Gone are the days when onboarding ended after a couple weeks. Everboarding is all about keeping the momentum going. This means creating an environment where learning and growth happen continuously. For talent development teams, this approach not only helps employees feel valued but also keeps us relevant in a rapidly evolving corporate environment. When we shift our focus to continuous growth, we can anticipate needs and address them before they become challenges.

Take action: Schedule a quarterly pulse survey or in-person check-in with employees to discuss their ongoing development goals and identify growth opportunities for the organization.

2. Collaboration Is a Game-Changer

Everboarding thrives on collaboration. It's not just about HR or talent development working in a silo; it's about building partnerships across the organization. Managers, employees, and the talent development team all have roles to play in this ongoing journey. By fostering a culture of collaboration, you not only support the development of employees but also position yourself as a strategic partner who understands the bigger picture and business goals.

Take action: Organize a cross-functional meeting with managers, HR, and the talent development team to align on shared goals for employee growth.

3. Data-Driven Decisions Make an Impact

In everboarding, data is your best friend. By leveraging analytics, you can track employee engagement, performance, and development needs more effectively. This data empowers you to make informed decisions that align with both individual aspirations and organizational objectives. When you harness the power of data, you demonstrate your strategic value and contribute to business outcomes.

Take action: Start tracking one key metric—such as employee engagement survey results or customer satisfaction data—and share the insights with your team to shape future initiatives.

4. Personalization Enhances Relevance

Every employee is unique—their development journey should be too. Everboarding allows you to tailor experiences to meet individual needs. By understanding each team member's preferences and aspirations, you can create personalized learning paths that resonate with them. This not only enhances their experience but also positions talent development as a key player in retaining top talent.

Take action: Have managers ask each employee during their next one-on-one about a skill or area they'd like to grow in, and begin tailoring their development plans accordingly.

5. Flexibility Is Essential

The business world is constantly changing, and so are the employee's needs. Everboarding embraces flexibility, allowing you to adapt your strategies in real time. Whether it's introducing new learning platforms, adjusting training programs, or responding to market shifts, your ability to pivot is crucial. This agility ensures that you stay ahead of the curve and continue to provide value to your organization.

Take action: Review your current training offerings and identify one area that you could adapt or modernize to better meet evolving business needs.

6. Fostering a Culture of Growth Empowers Employees

At the heart of everboarding is a culture of growth. By encouraging a mindset of continuous improvement, you empower employees to take ownership of their development. This doesn't just benefit them; it enhances your overall organizational culture, creating an environment where innovation and creativity thrive. When talent development teams champion this growth mindset, we solidify our role as catalysts for change within the business.

Take action: Highlight one recent success story within your organization that demonstrates continuous learning and share it in a newsletter to inspire others.

7. Strategic Alignment Is the Secret Sauce

Finally, everboarding aligns talent development initiatives with the organization's overall strategic goals. By understanding the business's direction and priorities, you can tailor your programs to support these objectives. This alignment showcases your value as a strategic partner who contributes to the bottom line, ensuring that talent development remains a priority in the business agenda.

Take action: Meet with a senior leader to discuss their point of view on how talent development initiatives can better align with one of the organization's strategic goals.

Closing Thoughts

Everboarding is far more than a continuation of traditional onboarding and this book intended to bring that idea to the forefront. By embracing this approach, talent development teams can remain relevant, strategic, and effective in today's dynamic work environment. We're not just onboarding new employees; we're fostering a culture of continuous growth, collaboration, and innovation.

As we move forward, let's keep these key takeaways in mind and continue to champion the everboarding philosophy in our organizations. Together, we can create a workplace where employees thrive, businesses succeed, and talent development shines as a vital component of that success.

Here's to making everboarding stick! May it guide you in your journey to change the workplace and shape the future.

Appendix
Case Studies

To bring the everboarding strategy to life, this appendix features three real-world case studies. Each is aligned to one phase of the everboarding journey—from onboarding foundations to manager-led development and employee-driven growth. All these stories showcase how organizations across different industries have applied everboarding principles to elevate their talent strategies. Whether you're starting fresh or refining an existing approach, these examples provide practical inspiration for putting everboarding into motion.

HERITAGE COMMUNITIES
Building a Better Employee Experience

Overview

Heritage Communities, a network of senior living communities, faced challenges with inconsistent onboarding and development practices across their locations, which led to high turnover and disengaged leadership teams. To address these challenges, the HR team—led by Debbie Petru—created a scalable "Hiring and Onboarding In-a-Box" program that emphasized leadership enablement and a consistent approach to the employee life cycle. This initiative, combined with everboarding strategies, resulted in measurable reductions in turnover rates and improved employee engagement.

Introduction

Background on Heritage Communities: Heritage Communities operates senior living communities that offer independent living, assisted living, memory care, and respite care in Nebraska, Iowa, Texas, and Arizona. With more than 20 years of experience and more than 15 locations, it has become a trusted name in senior care.

Overview of L&D at Heritage Communities: The human resources team at Heritage Communities consists of talent development and talent acquisition teams. These groups collaborate to ensure a streamlined employee life cycle, continually refining their processes to support the opening of new communities.

Challenge
Key issues:
- Each location independently managed onboarding, resulting in inconsistent practices.
- New locations experienced rapid employee turnover and leadership dissatisfaction.
- There wasn't a standardized preboarding or hiring process, which created a fragmented experience for employees.

Root causes:
- There wasn't a unified onboarding framework across communities.
- Leadership teams at new locations were left to figure out onboarding on their own.

Impact:
- Employees did not receive the support they needed during their crucial early days on the job.
- The talent acquisition team struggled to attract and retain talent due to inconsistent experiences.

Approach
Goals and objectives:
- Standardize the onboarding process across all locations.
- Enable leadership teams to provide consistent and supportive onboarding experiences.
- Create a sustainable and scalable program to support the rapid growth of new communities.

Strategies implemented:
- Developed the "Hiring and Onboarding In-a-Box" program to ensure leadership teams were equipped to manage employee development
- Designed everboarding initiatives to extend onboarding beyond the first few weeks
- Introduced training and resources tailored to the needs of leadership teams at new locations

Solution
Specific programs:
- Facilitated in-person leadership training at new locations, including trust-building exercises and role-specific learning paths
- Implemented a train-the-trainer model to empower leaders to deliver consistent general orientation experiences
- Developed a buddy program and Slack channels for peer collaboration across locations

Tools and technologies:
- Created a centralized intranet (SharePoint) for easy access to onboarding materials
- Standardized orientation road maps for all roles, including leadership-specific road maps

Partnerships:
- Collaborated with the marketing team to align preboarding strategies with employer branding

Outcome
Quantitative results:
- The overall turnover rate decreased by 2 percent.
- Turnover in the first 100 days dropped by 1 percent.
- There were significant improvements in nursing retention, with a 5.3 percent reduction in overall turnover and a 3.28 percent reduction in the first 100 days.
- Regional turnover reductions:
  - Central Nebraska: 8 percent overall; 6 percent in the first 100 days.
  - Omaha Metro (Iowa): 4 percent overall and in the first 100 days.
  - Southwest region (excluding Texas): 6 percent overall and 1 percent in the first 100 days.

Qualitative results:
- Leadership teams reported feeling better equipped to manage onboarding and training.
- Employees expressed greater confidence in their roles and alignment with Heritage Communities' values.

Lessons Learned
- A standardized approach to onboarding creates consistency and improves employee confidence.
- Leadership enablement is critical for the success of new communities.
- Ongoing observation and feedback ensure continuous improvement of onboarding practices.

Key Takeaways
- Standardizing onboarding and development processes reduces turnover and improves engagement.
- Extending onboarding into an everboarding strategy helps align with employees' life cycle stages.
- Investing in leadership training builds trust and ensures cultural alignment.

Conclusion
Debbie Petru's team transformed Heritage Communities' onboarding and employee development practices with the "Hiring and Onboarding In-a-Box" initiative. By focusing on leadership enablement, everboarding, and consistency, the company significantly reduced turnover rates and set a foundation for long-term success. This approach demonstrates the importance of aligning onboarding processes with an employee's life cycle to create a sustainable and engaging workplace culture.

DATA AXLE
Increasing Sales Performance With a Structured, Sustainable Path for Continuous Learning

Overview

Data Axle, a leading provider of data and marketing solutions, faced significant challenges in onboarding and training its sales team, which led to long ramp-up times and inconsistencies in sales performance. The introduction of a standardized training program—supported by tools like Highspot, Spekit, and Mindtickle—streamlined onboarding and ensured ongoing development for new and tenured employees. This approach, led by Jessica Jones and Amber Kraus, reduced time to productivity, improved sales alignment, and established a culture of continuous learning.

Introduction

Background on Data Axle: Data Axle is a trusted name in data and marketing, with more than 50 years of experience. The company provides solutions ranging from one-time-use consumer lists to advanced Connected TV (CTV) advertising services.

Overview of the LMS Business Unit: The LMS business unit primarily serves small to midsize businesses and reseller clients. Its sales team is responsible for offering a diverse portfolio of solutions, acting as consultants who align client goals with the right products. However, the complexity of the offerings and the varied client needs pose challenges for both new and experienced sales employees.

Challenge
Key issues:
- *A disjointed onboarding process:*
  - New hires spent six months with the talent development team before transitioning to sales managers. This resulted in gaps in role expectations and support.
  - Sales managers were minimally involved in onboarding, leading to misalignment and inconsistent practices.

- *A lack of ongoing development for tenured employees:*
  - Updates on new products and processes were communicated through emails and quick meetings without additional reinforcement.
  - Tenured employees struggled to absorb and apply new information, leading to inefficiencies and outdated practices.

Impact:
- Ramp-up times for new hires ranged from six to 24 months.
- Sales performance dropped significantly post-transition from the talent development team to sales managers.
- Misalignment between training and sales leadership created confusion and inefficiencies across teams.

Approach
Goals and objectives:
- Standardize onboarding across all sales teams.
- Involve sales managers in the onboarding and development process.
- Create a structured and sustainable path for continuous learning for both new and tenured employees.

Phased strategy:
- *Phase 1. Identify core challenges.*
  - Conducted interviews with sales managers to understand gaps in training and role expectations
  - Identified areas where managers and training teams were misaligned

- *Phase 2. Build standardized training programs.*
  - Introduced core training for universal products, services, and processes, followed by role-specific training
  - Reduced onboarding duration from six months to four weeks before transitioning to sales teams
  - Incorporated structured weekly meetings between managers and new hires for the first 90 days

- *Phase 3. Ensure sustainability and continuous improvement.*
  - Designed playbooks outlining the responsibilities of managers versus training teams
  - Leveraged Spekit to provide on-demand resources for processes and updates
  - Implemented a "SOS channel" for new hires to ask questions and address challenges

Solution
Onboarding improvements:
- Training courses in Mindtickle now launch in week 5 of onboarding.
- Managers and new hires collaborate weekly to identify gaps and enroll in refresher training as needed.
- The team removed the six-month graduation milestone and replaced it with ongoing milestones and certifications.

Ongoing development for tenured employees:
- Rolled out structured training for product updates, reinforced through Spekit guides and refresher courses
- Introduced tiered bonus structures (silver, gold, and platinum) to incentivize faster ramp-up times
- Required certifications and badges for selling certain services, ensuring mastery of key products

Tools and technology:
- Mindtickle for onboarding courses, sales metrics tracking, and bonus eligibility documentation
- Spekit for on-demand guides and support on specific processes
- Highspot for accessing playbooks and training guides

Outcome
Quantitative results:
- Reduced ramp-up time for new hires from six to 24 months to under six months
- Increased sales performance for new hires within their first 90 days
- Improved adoption of new processes and product knowledge among tenured employees

Qualitative results:
- Managers reported feeling more confident in supporting new hires.
- New hires expressed greater clarity in their roles and expectations, leading to improved team assimilation.
- Tenured employees noted better access to resources for ongoing learning and development.

Lessons Learned
- Manager involvement is critical to the success of onboarding and ongoing development.
- Continuous learning paths, supported by tools like Spekit, enhance knowledge retention and application.
- Replacing rigid milestones with flexible, ongoing certifications motivates employees to stay engaged.

Key Takeaways
- Standardizing onboarding reduces ramp-up time and ensures alignment across teams.
- Technology plays a key role in delivering just-in-time learning and reinforcing knowledge.
- Structuring manager-employee interactions during onboarding improves role clarity and team integration.

Conclusion
Jessica Jones and Amber Kraus's commitment to standardizing sales onboarding and ongoing development has set a strong foundation for sustained success. By involving managers, leveraging innovative tools, and focusing on continuous learning, Data Axle addressed its key challenges and empowered its sales teams to thrive in a complex and competitive market.

NOKIA
Equipping Employees With Robust Data Analytics Skills Through Innovative Workshop Design

Overview
As Nokia continues to innovate in the digital era, the organization has recognized the need to equip employees with robust data analytics skills to support data-driven decision making. Many employees had experience with basic tools like Excel but lacked the confidence or skills to transition to advanced analytics platforms like Python.

Challenge
Key issues:
- Provide foundational analytics training to employees from various backgrounds.
- Create a seamless transition from basic analytics tools (Excel) to more advanced ones (Python).

Solution
Nokia's L&D team, led by Steve Tadeo, identified an opportunity to address these challenges by designing a hands-on, three-day workshop centered on the Titanic dataset to explore descriptive, diagnostic, and inferential analytics, while leveraging both Excel and Python.

Structure of the workshop:
- **Descriptive analytics**
  - *Focus:* Summarize data to identify patterns and trends.
  - *Activities:* Calculate metrics (such as survival rates by gender and passenger class) and create visualizations (such as histograms and bar charts) to analyze passenger demographics.
  - *Tools:* Excel and Python
  - *Key outcome:* Participants gain skills in interpreting data to uncover surface-level insights.

- **Diagnostic analytics**
  - *Focus:* Explore relationships and understand causal factors behind trends.
  - *Activities:* Perform correlation analysis and hypothesis testing (such as testing the relationship between gender and survival), and create visualizations such as boxplots to compare variables such as fare distribution.
  - *Tools:* Excel and Python
  - *Key outcome:* Participants learn to identify and explain relationships between variables.

- **Inferential analytics**
  - *Focus:* Make predictions and draw conclusions from data.
  - *Activities:* Calculate confidence intervals for survival rates by groups, and build logistic regression models to predict survival likelihood based on variables like age, class, and gender.
  - *Tools:* Excel and Python
  - *Key outcome:* Participants develop the ability to use statistical models to make data-driven predictions.

Facilitator's perspective: Steve Tadeo's own career journey inspired the workshop's design. His transition from mechanical engineering to data science and learning analytics demonstrated the value of upskilling and embracing new tools like Tableau, Python, and SQL. Steve's story resonated with participants, motivating them to embrace growth and overcome challenges in their own data journeys.

Outcomes

- **Enhanced skills.** Participants gained confidence in their ability to handle both foundational and advanced analytics tasks, seamlessly transitioning from Excel to Python.
- **Increased data literacy.** Employees became better equipped to analyze data trends, identify insights, and apply them to solve real-world business problems.
- **Practical application.** By focusing on the Titanic dataset, participants learned how to apply analytics techniques in a meaningful and relatable context.
- **Cultural shift.** Nokia reinforced a culture of continuous learning and innovation by supporting employees in acquiring skills relevant to the future of work.

Conclusion

This case study highlights how Nokia addressed a critical organizational need for enhanced data analytics capabilities by creating an engaging, hands-on workshop. Through a structured, multiphase approach and the integration of both Excel and Python, employees gained practical, scalable skills to support Nokia's digital transformation.

Steve Tadeo's leadership and passion for analytics were instrumental in the program's success, underscoring the power of combining technical expertise with a commitment to lifelong learning.

References

ATD (Association for Talent Development). 2023. *Building a Strong Organizational Culture: The Role of the TD Function.* ATD Press.

Gallup. n.d. "How to Improve the Employee Experience." Gallup Workplace. gallup.com/workplace/323573/employee-experience-and-workplace-culture.aspx.

Garmus, B. 2022. *Lessons in Chemistry.* Doubleday.

Kim, D. 1999. *Introduction to Systems Thinking.* Pegasus Communications.

Scott, K. 2017. *Radical Candor: Be a Kick-Ass Boss Without Losing Your Humanity.* St. Martin's Press.

Thaler, R.H., and C.R. Sunstein. 2008. *Nudge: Improving Decisions About Health, Wealth and Happiness.* Yale University Press.

References

Index

In this index, *f* denotes figure and *t* denotes table.

A
accountability. *See* alignment charters
adaptability, 86
AI, 141–142
alignment, strategic, 147
alignment charters, 13–17
alignment meetings, 7–9
assets, for change, 81–82
    See also technology
autonomy, 73, 104

B
benchmarking, 136–138
BEST Feedback Model, 50
blended learning, 114
branding guidelines, 27
breaks, during onboarding, 30
Brown, A., 109, 122, 131
buddies, 46
Building a Strong Organizational Culture (ATD), xi
burnout, 58

C
capabilities, for change, 79–81
Carver, G., 75
cascading goals, 108
case studies, 150–161

change management, 72–73, 141–142
    See also MOCCA Change Management Methodology
coaching, 46, 111–112
    See also mentors; personal trainer method
collaboration and collaboration tools, 63–64, 111–112, 122, 146
    See also partnering
communication, 77–79, 138
    See also feedback
confidence, of managers, 86–87, 103
continuous learning mindsets, 79, 145
cross-role exposure, 120, 121–122
cultural contribution awards, 128
curated development pathways, 110–111, 123
    See also focused learning paths
current employees, everboarding and, 135–144

D
data and data analytics. *See* metrics and evaluations; Nokia case study
Data Axle, 102, 136
Data Axle case study, 154–158
development pathways, curated, 110–111, 123
    See also focused learning paths

development plans, 38, 139–141f
　See also AI; Data Axle case study
development progress reviews, 109
documentation, 95, 96
　See also metrics and evaluations

E

early mastery, pitfalls of, 57–59
element libraries, 27
emotional regulation, 86
employee engagement surveys, 109
employee personas, 36–39
employees. See current employees, everboarding and; new hire success
employee success
　autonomy and, 73, 104
　everboarding process and, 4–5
　factors limiting, 84
　feedback and, 8, 91
　hybrid learning programs and, 29–31
　manager motivation and, 75
　mental health awareness and, 31–33
　onboarding and, xiii, 21–22
　personas and, 36–39
　self-led learning and, 119
　technology use and, 80
　vision sharing and, 76–77
empowerment, 17, 38, 146, 147
　See also personal trainer method
engagement
　continuous learning mindsets, 145
　everboarding versus, 127
　levels of, 95, 104
　and retention strategies, 113
　See also employee engagement surveys

evaluations. See metrics and evaluations
everboarding
　about, vii–xi, 4f, 53
　benefits of, v–vi, xi–xii, 1, 89, 114
　challenges in beginning, vii–viii
　as compared to onboarding, ixf
　on-demand learning versus, 83
　and development of managers, x, 7
　early mastery and, 58–59
　engagement versus, 127
　factors impacting success of, vii, 3–5, 145–147
　phases of, 5–13
Excel, 159, 160, 161

F

FAQ channels, 125–126
feedback
　employee success and, 8, 91
　as enabler of change, 79
　manager tips about, 98
　by mentors, 111
　tools for, 108–109
　See also BEST Feedback Model; recognition
feedback training, 49–51
feedforward, 109
flexibility, 147
　See also change management
focused learning paths, 124–125
　See also curated development pathways
FOCUS Framework, 98–100
Ford, H., 72

G

goals and goal revision, 108

growth culture. *See* coaching; continuous learning mindsets; mentors; self-led learning

H
habit formation, 94, 95
   See also key performance indicators (KPIs); quality of work
Heritage Communities case study, 150–153
"Hiring and Onboarding In-a-Box" program, 150–153
Hoyle, L., 124
hybrid and remote teams, 29–31, 64, 125, 129

I
interviews, 90

J
Jones, J., 154

K
key performance indicators (KPIs), 90, 91, 94, 142
key results. *See* objectives and key results (OKRs)
Kim, D., 83
knowledge and resource curation, 123–124
knowledge sharing, 122
Kraus, A., 154
Kvarfordt, J., 140

L
learning advisory board charters, 26–29
learning advisory boards (LABs), 25–29, 33–34
learning content personalization, 39–41
learning curves, 91–92
learning management system (LMS), 10, 63, 109
learning playlists, 124
learning retention methods, 10, 11*f*
legacy knowledge, 122
lesson creation templates, 27
LMS. *See* learning management system (LMS)
LOPAFT Model, 140–141*f*

M
manager-driven recognition, 128
manager-led employee development
   alignment meetings for, 7–9
   competency in, 79–80
   ongoing support for, 107–115
   preparing managers for, 83–88
   recognition during, 132
   supporting and evaluating new-hire success, 89–105
   through knowledge and resource curation, 123
manager playbooks, 100–105
managers
   employee personas and, 38
   employee recognition and, 128, 130
   everboarding and development of, x, 7
   feedback tips for, 98
   mental health awareness and, 32
   motivation of, 75, 86–87
   and opposition to mentors, 47
   and preparation for manager-led employee development, 83–88
   responsibilities of, 13, 15, 23
   securing involvement of, 69–82

strategies to improve confidence of, 86–87, 103
and support of postgrad training, vi–vii
training team partnership with, 7–8
manager– talent development team touchpoints, 110
manager toolkits, 87
mastery, early, 57–59
measurement. *See* metrics and evaluations
mental health awareness, 31–33
mentor application forms, 47–49
mentors
    development framework for, 111–112
    employee personas and, 38
    knowledge sharing and, 122
    preparation of, 45–51
    responsibilities of, 23, 33
metrics and evaluations
    alignment charters and, 15–16
    on capabilities for change, 80
    early mastery and, 57
    empowerment through, 146
    manager playbooks and, 104–105
    new-hire data and assessment, 90–97
    to track recognition, 129
    See also key performance indicators (KPIs); Nokia case study
milestones
    benefits of using, 63, 64
    celebrating achievement of, 56–57, 138–139
    as design for sustained development, 59–63
    role of technology in supporting, 63–64

    types of, 55–56, 61–62
mindsets, continuous learning, 79, 145
Mindtrickle, 154, 156, 157
MOCCA Change Management Methodology, 74–82
motivation, by managers, 75, 86–87
motivation, for change, 74–75

N

new-hire mentoring programs, 46–47, 49–50
new hire success, 89–105
    See also employee success; onboarding
Nokia case study, 159–161
nudge theory, 120, 121*t*

O

objectives and key results (OKRs), 41, 94–95, 98–99
onboarding
    about, 5–7
    breaks during, 30
    everboarding as compared to, ix*f*
    factors impacting success of, v, vii–viii, xi, xiii, 21–22, 57
    mental health awareness during, 32
    personalization of, 35–44
    recognition during, 132
    traditional view of, 53–54
    See also "Hiring and Onboarding In-a-Box" program
onboarding, standardization of. *See* case studies
onboarding platforms, 63
on-demand learning, 83
one-on-one best practices, 97–98
    See also FOCUS Framework
optics, for change, 75–77

organizational culture
    employee recognition and, 128, 130
    factors impacting, xi, 21
    knowledge sharing and, 122
    mentors and, 46

P

partnering
    activities to support, 1–3
    learning playlists and, 124
    for stackable learning, 111
    See also collaboration and collaboration tools; managers; mentors
peer coaches, 46
peer recognition, 128
performance-based recognition, 128
performance-focused mentoring programs, 46, 49
performance improvement plans (PIPs), 7, 84, 139
performance management support, 107–115
performance management tools, 63
Pernicek, T., 131–132
personalization, 35–44, 146
    See also curated development pathways; focused learning paths
personal trainer method, 84–85
Petru, D., 150
PIPs. *See* performance improvement plans (PIPs)
podcasts, 30
postgrad training, vi–vii
    See also everboarding
professional development, vi
progress. *See* development progress reviews; goals and goal revision
Python, 159, 160, 161

Q

quality of work, 95–96
quick mastery, pitfalls of, 57–59

R

Radical Candor (Scott), 49
recency bias, 91–92
recognition, 127–133
recognition platforms, 64, 130
refinement program, 9–13
    See also self-led learning
reinforcement strategies, 10, 11*t*
    See also milestones
remote teams. *See* hybrid and remote teams
resilience, 75
resources. *See* assets, for change; knowledge and resource curation; support systems; technology
retention and engagement strategies, 113
role reversals, 10

S

scalability of development, 104, 114, 141, 143
Scott, K., 49
self-awareness, 86
self-led learning, 10–13, 119–126, 132–133
skill gaps, addressing of, 140–141*f*
skill mastery and learning, 128
stackable learning, 110, 111
stretch assignments, 112
style guides, 27
succession planning, 112–114
success teams, 22–24
    See also learning advisory boards (LABs)

support systems, 21–34, 100, 107–115
   See also coaching; *manager entries*; mentors; partnering; retention and engagement strategies; technology
surveys, 109, 136–138, 142, 145
Sustained Development Assessment Quiz, 59*f*–61*f*
systems, defined, 83

T
Tadeo, S., 159, 161
tailored development programs, 113–114
talent development teams
   availability of, 31
   factors impacting success of, 89
   recognition system roles for, 131–132
   responsibilities of, 5, 13, 14–15, 23, 83
   and role in new-hire success, 90–97
   and role in performance management support, 107–115
   See also learning advisory boards (LABs)
talent pool integration, 112–114
targeted learning resources, 110–111
technology, 63–64, 80, 85, 141–142
   See also learning management system (LMS)
tenured employees, everboarding and, 135–144
Top Gun–style onboarding program, 40–41
training schedules, 30, 34, 42–43
turnover, 58, 152

U
understanding, one-on-one best practices and addressing, 99

V
virtual training, postgrad training as, vi–vii, 30–31
vision sharing. *See* optics, for change

About the Author

Amber Watts has more than a decade of experience in talent development and sales enablement, specializing in everboarding, change management, and talent strategy. She is currently the founder and CEO of Radical GrowthWorks.

Passionate about empowering people to grow and bridging the gap between strategy and execution, Amber builds scalable systems that drive learning, leadership, and business growth. She challenges conventional thinking, fosters continuous development, and helps organizations create cultures in which employees and businesses thrive.

Amber holds a BS in business management and leadership and certifications in coaching and virtual training design. Her work has earned numerous accolades; she was recognized as an Emerging Training Leader by *Training* magazine (2019) and awarded a Stevie Award for Sales Training/Coaching Program of the Year (2020) and an Excellence in Learning Leadership from the ATD Nebraska Chapter (2023).

About the Author

About ATD

atd The Association for Talent Development (ATD) is the world's largest association dedicated to those who develop talent in organizations. Serving a global community of members, customers, and international business partners in more than 100 countries, ATD champions the importance of learning and training by set-ting standards for the talent development profession.

Our customers and members work in public and private organizations in every industry sector. Since ATD was founded in 1943, the talent development field has expanded significantly to meet the needs of global businesses and emerging industries. Through the Talent Development Capability Model, education courses, certifications and credentials, memberships, industry-leading events, research, and publications, we help talent development professionals build their personal, professional, and organizational capabilities to meet new business demands with maximum impact and effectiveness.

One of the cornerstones of ATD's intellectual foundation, ATD Press offers insightful and practical information on talent development, training, and professional growth. ATD Press publications are written by industry thought leaders and offer anyone who works with adult learners the best practices, academic theory, and guidance necessary to move the profession forward.

We invite you to join our community. Learn more at **TD.org**.

www.ingramcontent.com/pod-product-compliance
Ingram Content Group UK Ltd.
Pitfield, Milton Keynes, MK11 3LW, UK
UKHW021846140426
5217IPUK00022B/1616